WONDER WOMEN *of the* BIBLE

HEROES OF YESTERDAY WHO INSPIRE US TODAY

BRENDA POINSETT

NEW HOPE PUBLISHERS
Birmingham, Alabama

New Hope® Publishers
P. O. Box 12065 Birmingham, AL 35202-2065
www.newhopepublishers.com
A Division of WMU ™

First printing 2007.
Printed in the United States of America.

Library of Congress Cataloging-in-Publication Data

Poinsett, Brenda.
Wonder women of the Bible : heroes of yesterday who inspire us today / Brenda Poinsett.
p. cm.
Includes bibliographical references.
ISBN-13: 978-1-59669-094-3 (sc)
1. Women in the Bible--Biography. 2. Bible--Biography. I. Title.
BS575.P66 2007
220.9'2082--dc22
2007009945

ISBN-13: 978-1-59669-094-3

ISBN-10: 1-59669-094-1

N074142 • 0807 • 5M1

DEDICATION

To

my sisters,

Linda Spires Cochran

and

Judith Spires Mills,

who definitely qualify as "wonder women."

CONTENTS

Part IV She Did What?

Part V She Felt How?

ACKNOWLEDGMENTS

There wouldn't be a book about the Bible's *Wonder* Women if it weren't for Rebecca England, formerly an editor with New Hope Publishers. She recognized the potential of this topic when she peeked in my Web site and saw where I gave presentations about these interesting women. This is the second time Rebecca has spotted something publication worthy from my Web site. The other was my book *Can Martha Have a Mary Christmas?*

Rebecca's interest in the topic encouraged me as did the invitation of the women of the Galilee Baptist Church of Decatur, Illinois. They invited me to speak twice on the Bible's *Wonder* Women. Many churches have invited me back to speak a second time but this church holds the distinction of being the only one to ask me back to give the exact same speech.

I also appreciate the women of the First Baptist Church of Viburnum, Missouri, for giving me the opportunity to orally develop the topic beyond a speech. For me, there's nothing like face-to-face dialogue with a group of interested women to enhance content and get the creative juices flowing.

But once the creative juices began flowing, there was still the discipline of getting the material written down, and for that I needed prayer. I appreciate the prayers of Mary Rose Fox, Trish Rogers, Cathleen Ingle Weber, Debbie Hawkins, and Jan Turner. I also appreciate the prayers and encouraging words of my husband, Bob Poinsett.

Another need I had was having time to write. I thank my sisters, Linda Spires Cochran and Judith Spires Mills, for being flexible in the scheduling of care for our elderly mother. In fact, Judy took over my turn to care for Mom in January 2007 so I could finish the manuscript. Seeing how they care for Mom is one reason why they rank as "*wonder* women" in my estimation. They're the best!

While Rebecca has gone on to other life adventures, my relationship continues with New Hope through their new managing editor, Joyce Dinkins. I appreciate her belief in this topic, her patience with me, and most importantly to you the reader, her editing skills. To Joyce and to editors Cathy Butler and Carolyn Stanford Goss, page designers Freda Souter and Sherry Hunt, as well as the other members of the New Hope staff, I say, "Thank you. I count it a privilege to be associated with you."

INTRODUCTION

I'm a *wonder* woman. Are you?

I wonder about life, about God, and about the future. I wonder why things happen—sometimes too much so! Intrigued by the behavior of people, I wonder why people do what they do. One thing that has always interested me is their fascination with superheroes.

In recent years, we've had a rash of superheroes—Spider-Man, Batman, Daredevil, the Hulk, Cat Woman, Elektra, Lara Croft, and Blade. Like Superman, Captain Marvel, and Wonder Woman who came before them, most are comic book characters that leaped off the page and onto our movie and television screens. With their phenomenal strength and unusual abilities, they can scale heights, fly through the air, and defeat any enemy no matter how formidable. Judging by the sales of theater tickets, videos, DVDs, and hero-related paraphernalia, many people are fascinated by them. One explanation for the fascination may have to do with the times in which we live. Because things are so chaotic and unsettled, we want a superhero who can solve world problems. When we watch stories of superheroes, we can step into a world of sharp contrasts where attractive, strong men and women triumph over all odds. For a couple of hours we can live in an environment where might triumphs over evil.

Or maybe the explanation has to do with our stress-filled lives. As we watch, we secretly hope some of the superhero's magic will rub off on us so that we may exercise more control in our own lives and experience more triumphs. My son Jim expressed this wish when he was just seven years old. When things got frustrating for him, he said, "Why doesn't Jesus give us the power to turn into Captain Marvel?"

Jim's nephew, our grandson Christophe, thought he could take it a step further and actually turn into a superhero. As we sorted clothes, four-year-old Christophe spotted a coiled clothesline rope—one that I had been waiting for the "Superman" in my life to put up outside. "What's this, Grandma?"

I explained that it was a rope to hang wet clothes on to dry outside.

He said, "Can I play with it?"

I said, "Well, sure," and wondered what he had in mind.

Outside, he stood about eight feet from a tree and began throwing the rope toward it. After numerous throws, the rope wrapped itself around a limb. Then using the rope, Christophe started pulling himself up into the tree. He looked at me, smiled and proudly proclaimed, "Look, Grandma. Spider-man!"

I marveled that he could so readily identify with Spider-man and believe he could replicate his ability. It never occurred to him that he couldn't, but it occurs to me. I'm a realist. When it comes to identifying, I need someone I can connect with, someone in circumstances like mine who uses weapons that are also available to me.

Maybe that is why instead of being fascinated with superheroes, I'm fascinated with some women of the Bible—real women, not computer-generated women, who responded to life and to God in ways that I can identify with. Just as Christophe threw his rope into the tree, I tossed out my rope of learning and lassoed some biblical women I can profit from knowing. In various ways, they teach me, encourage me, inspire me, and create wonder in me. Over time, as I connected with these women, a list began forming in my head—a list that I affectionately refer to as "the *wonder* women of the Bible."

Making the list

I didn't intentionally set out to make this list. I didn't sit down one day with a pencil in my hand, chew on the eraser and think, *Who are the women in the Bible that I could admire or relate to?* Rather, these women jumped off the pages of the Bible at different junctures in my life when I needed them.

I didn't need all of them at the same time. Sometimes the need was major, sometimes it was minor, nevertheless, each woman stuck in my memory and became part of my list because she met a need.

- When faced with out-of-the-ordinary circumstances, I needed examples of women who could do the extraordinary—women of daring and courage. Their stories reminded me that real women can do unusual things and their bravery inspired me to be more courageous and confident.

- When I noticed acts of kindness and mercy going unappreciated or unacknowledged, I needed heroines who were known for their unselfishness and their loving acts of kindness. I needed to learn how a woman can live life in the loving, graceful spirit of Jesus.
- Life is not simple and much is expected of women. We have many roles. When I wondered if I could handle all my roles, I looked at Bible women who were given many roles by God and were empowered to accomplish them.
- Besides having many roles, women are influenced and molded by cultural and religious expectations. When I've felt stifled by those expectations, I needed stories of women who stepped outside of the expected and did something unexpected—sometimes even something incredible. Even when I didn't want to imitate their behavior, their stories stirred up a sense of possibility within me.
- As we deal with the roles and expectations of life and encounter disappointments that come with living, our sense of wonder can erode. I don't want that to happen. I want to delight in life, in nature, in God, and in His Son, so when I felt my joy slipping away, I connected with women whose stories nurtured my sense of wonder.

How about you? Have you encountered some dips and twists in life, some that have called for courage, tenacity, or perseverance? Do you need some heroes, some role models, to show you how to respond to challenges or to encourage you to hang tough in your stress-filled life? If you have ever doubted your ability, lacked courage, or felt undervalued, overlooked, or limited in what you can do, then I invite you to look at the Bible's *wonder* women with me. Throw out your lasso, draw each woman's story close to you, and see what a difference knowing her will make in your life.

Part I

ISN'T SHE STRONG?

The phrase I most often associate with superheroes is "able to leap over tall buildings in a single bound." It comes from a description of Superman. Obviously, this kind of ability is what sets superheroes apart from mere mortals. The Wonder Woman of the comics and TV that many of us grew up with is the female counterpart to Superman in many obvious ways. Fully capable of performing Superman-like (or Superwoman-like) feats and armed with super strength and magic items such as bullet-deflecting bracelets, she also carries a magic lasso that can force people to tell the truth.

I don't know any women in the Bible who have superhuman power like Superman or Wonder Woman, but I do know women who had unusual courage and who, empowered by God, did extraordinary things. In fact, the things they did were so unusual that I can't help but give them a "wonder woman" label.

These women were not miracle workers nor did they have abilities that other people don't possess; however, their examples speak to me because of their unusual daring and courage. They are remarkable because of what they accomplished. They were strong, brave women who played pivotal roles at crucial times in the history of God's people. If it hadn't been for them, no telling what would have happened to God's people. They were truly heroes, and there's something about each one we can emulate; we can connect because they are women like us.

Chapter One

RAHAB

Unflappable Action Saved a Nation

Joshua 2:1–21; 6:16–25; Hebrews 11:30–31; James 2:25

As a *wonder* woman, I'm interested in how we select our heroes, those people we might want to emulate in some way. For me, some kind of identification with the person is usually involved; there must be something about the person that I can relate to.

Perhaps surprisingly, the first *wonder* woman that we are going to look at is not someone I readily identified with at first and for good reason. She was a prostitute!

Whenever I read her story in the Bible, I didn't connect with her because our lives were nothing alike, but then I began talking about my *Wonder* Women list. After sharing it with one group, a frail woman who looked about 40 years old said, "Don't you think Rahab ought to be on that list?"

"Is she on yours?"

"Oh, yes, she is."

I promised her that I would give Rahab some consideration and went back to the Bible to study her story. Let's throw our lassos at her story to find out if she is indeed a *wonder* woman.

Who was Rahab?

Rahab was a single woman and a business owner living in the land of Canaan. She owned Rahab's Inn, built on the walls that surrounded Jericho, an important Canaanite city. Jericho was fortified with two walls built around it. One wall was built inside the other, and the walls were about ten to twelve feet apart. The walls were so sturdy and strong that people built houses on the walls, by laying planks out across them for the floor. People in these houses could see what was going on in the city and also what was going on in the countryside.

Rahab's inn was one of the wall structures. It was a popular place, with people coming and going at all hours. The fact that she was a prostitute or harlot may have contributed to the brisk business.

As I read and studied Rahab's story in the Bible, my imagination took over. I could see her doing business as usual one day when two strangers arrived. As she talked with the strangers, she learned they were with a group camped by the Jordan River. They called themselves Israelites. At one time Moses had been their leader, but now Joshua was. In fact he had sent them to town.

The wheels of Rahab's mind started turning. *Israelites? Moses? Sent to town? Could these men be from the nation we have heard so much about? The nation whose god parted the*

Red Sea? The nation who killed some kings east of the Jordan? The group that has many Canaanites scared?

Rahab had heard all kinds of tales, some true and some untrue, from people who stayed at her inn. She thought, *if these men are from this nation and they have been sent to town by their leader, then that means they are probably getting ready to attack us. Oh, dear, this must mean they are spies!*

Toughened by years in the hospitality business, Rahab didn't flinch at this realization. She looked at the men and asked, "Are you spies?"

They looked at each other, hesitated, and then one finally said, "Yes, we are."

"Why are you here in Jericho?"

"Years ago, our people were slaves in Egypt. Our God provided us an escape through Moses' leadership. Moses said he was taking us to the Promised Land. After being slaves and encountering many difficulties along the way, our people had a hard time cooperating with Moses, so they wandered around for 40 years. They didn't have enough faith to conquer the Promised Land. You see, even though God promised us land, other people were already living there. The promise was going to have to be claimed. Now we are ready to do that. Just before Moses died, our people were finally ready, and Moses turned the leadership over to Joshua."

Rahab interrupted. "Wait a minute. This Promised Land you speak of? That's not our land, is it? You don't mean Canaan, do you?"

"I'm afraid so."

"So you are here to check out the city and the layout of the land to help Joshua plan his strategy?"

The men meekly nodded.

Rahab told them, "Jericho will not be an easy place to defeat. I'm sure you noticed as you came in that our city is elevated about 40 feet above the surrounding plains and it is enclosed by two walls, the walls on which my inn sits. I'm sure you also noticed the city gates as you came in. You were fortunate that they were opened today. The gates are closed any time the city feels threatened, and of course, the gates are closed at night. When the gates are closed, we feel safe and secure. In fact, we could probably resist an invading army almost indefinitely as long as our water and food supply lasts."

"Yes, we're aware of Jericho's advantages. That's one reason Joshua sent us, to see if we could uncover any kind of weakness that would be in our favor. We need to conquer Jericho if we are to move out into the rest of Canaan."

As he was talking, Rahab noticed it was starting to get dark outside. As she glanced out the window, she saw what looked like some of the king's men coming toward her house. (One advantage of having a dwelling built on the walls was that it gave the person inside the building a good view.)

She said to the Israelite spies, "I don't mean to alarm you but I think your presence in Jericho has been noticed. I hope I'm wrong but I think the king's men are looking for you. Quick, let me take you up on the roof. I can hide you there under some stalks of flax that I'm drying. I weave in my spare time."

Where are they?

So unflappable was Rahab that she rushed the spies up to the roof, covered them, and was back to answer the knock at the door in a jiffy without losing her cool. So far, this was just one of many "interesting" experiences she had had as an innkeeper.

Speaking authoritatively, the king's men demanded, "We believe you have some men in your house that have come to spy out our country. Hand them over at once."

"What men? I have people coming to my inn all the time."

"The men who were strangers and who were in the market place earlier. Many people saw them and think they are Israelites—you know, those people who have the God that dried up the Red Sea and who killed Sihon and Og, the two Amorite kings. Some citizens complained to the king about these strangers, and he's alarmed. He's afraid the Israelites will try to conquer Jericho."

"What did the men look like?"

"They were of medium height with dark hair and beards. They were heavily tanned as if they spent most of their time out of doors. Their clothes were worn, as if they had traveled a long way."

"Oh, I know the ones you mean. Yes, they were here earlier. They left just awhile ago. They wanted to get going before the city gate closed. They didn't tell me where they were going, but if you start after them quickly, I'm sure you can overtake them."

The king's men left immediately, and as Rahab shut the door behind them, she leaned against it and pondered what just happened. She asked herself, Why did I cover up for them? I could be killed if I were caught lying to the king's men. The men I hid are spies, after all. They are planning to enter our city and destroy it if they can. If?

Who am I kidding? If their God is who they say He is, then we won't have a chance. We'll all be destroyed.

Slowly she climbed the steps to the roof. As she did, it became clear to her that the god of the spies was the true God. Even though the conviction seemed to come suddenly, she realized it had been growing in her for some time. She was so relieved; she had always been confused about the many Canaanite gods. There were El (aka "Father Bull"), Asherah, Baal, and others. Stories about them were filled with brutality and immorality. Rahab was weary of religious rites that included prostitutes, child sacrifice, and snake worship. She wanted something cleaner; she wanted a holy God who was real and who responded to His people.

Once on the roof, she pulled back the flax and said to the spies, "I know that God has given you the land." And then she also said something very startling—and something that would be very helpful to Joshua. She said, "Everyone in the country is terrified of you" (Joshua 2:9c GNT).

She acknowledged to them, "The LORD your God is God in heaven above and here on earth" (Joshua 2:11 GNT).

She was so confident in the God of heaven and earth being the God of the Israelites that she believed God's people would be successful in conquering Jericho. This meant the entire city would be destroyed. That was the way war was. She wanted to protect her family. Surely, she thought, protecting these spies at great risk to myself should mean something. Doesn't one kindness deserve a kindness in return?

She said to the spies, "You've said today that your God is *the* God, and I believe you. Now please swear by *Him* that you will treat my family as kindly as I have treated you. Promise me that you will save my father and mother, my brothers and sisters, and all their children! Don't let us be killed!"

Grateful to Rahab for having saved their lives, the spies pledged to save her and her family. They said to her, "May God take our lives if we don't do as we say!"

There might have been a little lingering doubt about her reliability because they insisted the promise was only good if she kept silent about them and their agreement. They said, "If you do not tell anyone what we have been doing, we promise you that when the LORD gives us this land, we will treat you well" (Joshua 2:14 GNT).

They wanted to also make sure they would remember which house was hers. To guarantee her safety, she was to tie a red thread in a window of her house. She was also to make sure that her family remained in the house throughout the invasion. They said, "As long as the red thread remained visible, everyone in the house will be safe."

After they made their agreement, Rahab urged them to get going. "Go into the hill country. Hide there for three days. By that time the king's men will have stopped looking. Then you can go on your way."

With a rope, she lowered the two men down to the ground. Then she attached a red thread to the window and waited. Rahab waited confidently and hopefully—she had become a woman of faith.

Back at camp

The spies followed Rahab's suggestion and hid in the mountains for three days. When they saw the king's search party head back to Jericho, they returned to camp.

They gave Joshua the good news—the news they learned from Rahab: "All the people there are terrified of us." Joshua smiled as he heard the news for he remembered what Moses told him. He said that God had promised, "This very day I will begin to put the terror and fear of you on all the nations under heaven. They will hear reports of you and will tremble and be in anguish because of you" (Deuteronomy 2:25 NIV). Time to go to war!

Following God's instructions, for six days, once a day, they marched around Jericho. Seven priests led them, marching in front of the Ark that contained the Ten Commandments and bearing trumpets of rams' horns. Each day, they marched around the city in silence. The Jericho residents stood on their city walls or looked out their windows at the marchers. They had no horses, no heavy machines to batter down the city walls, no armor to turn back the arrows of the soldiers perched on the city walls. The invaders did not appear dangerous yet something eerie was going on. The people of Jericho were completely unnerved by the actions of the Israelites. "The gates of Jericho were kept shut and guarded to keep the Israelites out. No one could enter or leave the city" (Joshua 6:1 GNT).

On the seventh day, the Israelites marched again. They started early in the morning and circled the city in silence seven times and then gave a loud shout. At the same time, the priests blew the rams' horn, and this resulted in one powerful noise, so powerful the city walls collapsed. "Then all the army went straight up the hill into the city and captured it" (Joshua 6:20 GNT). They worked through the city killing everyone in their path. The main barrier to conquering the Promised Land was destroyed.

That was Rahab's story. What do you think? Should she be a *wonder* woman? Many others have esteemed her.

Rahab the Hero

Joshua said to the two men who had been spies, "Go to Rahab's house, and bring her and her family out as you promised." So they went and brought Rahab out, along with her father and mother, her brothers and sisters, and their slaves. They were all safe; Rahab's actions had saved both a nation and her family.

The Israelites made a place for Rahab and her kin near their camp but it wasn't long until the camps combined. Rahab left a life of prostitution behind and married Salmon, who may have been one of the two spies. The Bible says "her descendants have lived in Israel to this day" (Joshua 6:25 GNT), meaning many people can claim her as their ancestor. Among those are Boaz (the man who married Ruth—Matthew 1:5), King David (Matthew 1:6), and Jesus (Matthew 1:16). Rabbis who can do so have proudly traced their ancestry to her. "Jewish tradition teaches that Rahab became the ancestor of no less than eight prophets, including Jeremiah."[1]

Rahab is also admired by New Testament writers. James cites her as a great example of the good works which demonstrate faith. "She was put right with God through her actions, by welcoming the Israelite spies and helping them escape by a different road" (James 2:25 GNT).

Herbert Lockyer has called Rahab's faith "gloriously daring . . . To hide spies was a crime punishable with death . . . Yet with a calm demeanor, and without the slightest trace of inner agitation, she met them [the king's men] and succeeded in setting them out on a false trail. By her act Rahab was actually betraying her own country, and for such treason certain death would have been hers had she been found out."[2]

She is one of only two women listed in the honor roll of faith in Hebrews 11. "By faith the harlot Rahab perished not with them that believed not, when she had received the spies with peace" (Hebrews 11:31 KJV). William Barclay has said that when Rahab protected the spies "there seemed not one chance in a million that the children of Israel could capture Jericho. These nomads from the desert had no artillery and no siege-engines. It must have seemed fantastically improbable that they could ever breach the walls of Jericho and storm the city. Yet Rahab believed—and staked her whole future on the belief—that God would make the impossible possible . . . When commonsense pronounced the situation hopeless she had the uncommon sense to see beyond the situation."[3]

And to think I did not at first have her on my *wonder* women list! I'd say "Shame on me!" except that would disprove the point I'd tried to make at the beginning of the chapter. For someone to be a person I want to emulate, I need to identify with her in some way. I'm happy to say that happened when I reconsidered Rahab's story.

Connecting with Rahab

The most remarkable thing about Rahab is her faith. She exercised faith; she just didn't talk about it. I've always needed women to inspire me in this area. I did not receive the gift of faith that Paul describes in 1 Corinthians 12:9

so I have to nurture my faith along. This is one reason why the women in this book mean so much to me. Their stories strengthen my faith and help me look for possibilities where I don't see them.

Rahab's story also reminds us that we don't have to be perfect to be used by God. Being a prostitute didn't keep God from using her. While I can't identify with her lifestyle choice, I understand wrong decisions, regrets and mistakes, and her story reminds me that God can still use me. That's why Rahab was a hero to the frail forty-year-old I mentioned at the beginning of this chapter. She had made some mistakes, some really serious ones in her life, and Rahab's story encouraged her to think that God may have life-changing plans for her too.

Because of that, Rahab's story is a good one for us to begin this book with. Otherwise, the title *Wonder Women* might give you the idea that they are perfect women who lived perfect lives—now those would be women I could never identify with! Not all the heroes in the book lived exemplary lives. Rahab's story and theirs show us that even if we falter, even if we are sometimes bad, we are not canceled out by God.

With the challenges around us, with the many cultural influences we deal with, with being women who want to serve the Lord, we sometimes lose heart like the Israelites, but Rahab reminds us that the God who worked in her life wants to work in ours, too. And that knowledge inspires wonder in me. Does it inspire you?

Becoming a *wonder* woman

One Jewish rabbi called Rahab a righteous prostitute. What do you think he meant by that? Can a prostitute be righteous?

How crucial was Rahab's action to the success of the Israelites in conquering Jericho?

What kinds of things cause you to lose heart? What encourages you?

What about our culture pulls you down? What do you think caused Rahab to go counter to her culture?

What connection do faith and action have? Can you have one without the other?

What encouragement can ordinary women receive from Rahab's extraordinary action?

How do you select your heroes? What must be true about a person before you relate to them?

Chapter Two

DEBORAH

Iron Chariots Couldn't Keep Her Away

Judges 4 and 5

As a *wonder* woman, I've also asked myself this question as I throw out that truth-seeking lasso: Can you be a strong woman and serve the Lord? Can you be articulate, direct, assertive, and bold within the Christian community?

You may be puzzled that I even raise the question. In your church, men and women have equal say and equal standing. Or your answer may be like one woman's answer to me when I was thinking out loud. She said, "Of course, you can. Women's ministries really need strong women." Well, I have been strong and continue to be strong in women's ministries, but sometimes I've wanted more. I have felt I had a strength that I wasn't allowed to use. There have been times when I wanted to exert leadership about something I saw needed attention. A few times, I felt my church was going against a biblical principle and I wanted to speak up. Many times, I simply wanted to have some input, to be a part of the whole, but something in the attitude toward women held me back.

How about you? What is your natural bent? Do you ever feel you have an asset that you can't quite use fully? I'm naturally a bold, articulate, and direct woman. So was Deborah. Since I am that kind of woman, I'm grateful for her help in figuring out when and where I could be a strong woman.

Who was Deborah?

Deborah lived in the time of the judges, after Joshua had settled God's people in the Promised Land but before they had a king. As spectacular as Joshua's leadership was, the Israelites did not drive out all of Canaan's occupants as God had instructed them to do. Neither did the various tribes of Israel unite and work together. The Israelites were attracted to the gods their neighbors worshiped, and at times they worshiped those gods, too. When they did—when they were disobedient to God's commands—trouble came upon them.

When the oppression became unbearable, the people would cry out to God for a deliverer, and He would send a judge (a military leader) to rescue them. The judge got them out of trouble and then the people would be obedient for awhile, but eventually they would lapse back into ignoring God's commands. Oppression would again follow, and eventually they would cry out again to God for a deliverer. Each time, God was merciful and sent someone to rescue them. One of those deliverers was Deborah.

Besides being a military deliverer, Deborah was also a judge in the way judges today are. She settled disputes and dispensed wisdom. People came from far and wide to seek her help in resolving problems. This didn't seem to be an appointed role or an elected position; rather the people recognized in Deborah a godly woman of wisdom and integrity, someone they could trust with their concerns.

Her other roles may have contributed to her wisdom. She was a homemaker, the wife of Lappidoth, a prophetess, a singer, and a poet. As a wife, she knew the ins and outs of compromise. As a prophetess, she was aware of God's will, what He wanted for his people and how He expected them to live.

Like their male counterparts, prophetesses were God's spokespersons. They were conduits for God's messages. They heard from God and then they communicated His will to the people. As a singer and a poet, Deborah may have been particularly sensitive to spiritual matters and also adept in articulating what God wanted and expected.

Prophets and prophetesses were not only God's spokespersons, they were also seers. They could see things other people missed. In particular, Deborah could see that if God's people continued to live the way they were living, they would be destroyed by the more powerful Canaanites who still lived among them.

Her counseling "office" was under a palm tree between Ramah and Bethel in the hill country of Ephraim, where olive and palm trees flourished. In fact her office tree became known as "the Palm of Deborah." It was there that "the Israelites came to her to have their disputes decided" (Judges 4:5 NIV).

If we knew nothing else about Deborah—if we stopped the narrative right here, we would have to conclude that she was a remarkable woman because of the patriarchal nature of ancient Israelite society. Men made the decisions. The father of the family or clan reigned supreme, and women were legally dependent on their fathers and husbands. Women were viewed as property, not as persons who could think, who could respond, and who had rights. Choices were made for and about women's lives without their input. You can see how extreme this could be by reading the rest of the Book of Judges and noting how abominably women were sometimes treated.

In a time when the opinion of women didn't count, Deborah's did. She was a strong person whose wisdom was highly valued, but as remarkable as her wisdom was, that's not why I think of her as a *wonder* woman. It was her willingness to go up against 900 iron chariots to rescue her people.

Daring Deborah

After the Israelites had been rescued by the judge, Ehud, as described in Judges 3:12–30, they again disobeyed God's commands and worshiped other gods (Judges 4:1). As a result, they were punished. King Jabin and the Canaanites oppressed them. Their vineyards were destroyed, their women dishonored, and their children killed. For 20 years the oppression went on—and 20 years is a long time. Why hadn't anybody done anything?

Part of the reason may have been that the Israelites wanted God's blessing but they also wanted to live life their way. A kind of "Wild West" atmosphere prevailed, and everyone did what was right in their own eyes. To obey God meant putting restrictions on the way they lived. They may have resisted the restraints and hoped things would eventually work out; it would just take time.

Or perhaps the reason was fear. They were afraid of King Jabin's capable general, Sisera, and the powerful weapons of the Canaanites. The situation got so treacherous that "caravans no longer went through the land, and travelers used the back roads" (Judges 5:6 GNT).

Their weapons alone would have terrified the Israelites. The Canaanites had 900 iron chariots (Judges 4:3a), and that many armored chariots suggests a huge standing army. In addition, each chariot would have been manned by crack archers with long-range bows. The soldiers who walked along beside the chariots were equipped with iron spears and shields, and they wore protective iron helmets and coats of mail.

The Israelites were not well armed and had no chariots. Instead of iron spears and shields, they had bronze and copper daggers and swords, slings and short-range bows and arrows. Their wooden shields were leather covered; they had no armor.

When others might have been paralyzed with fear, Deborah wasn't. She believed that God would rescue His people. When the people finally had enough and cried out to the Lord for help, Deborah was ready to act. She sent for Barak, the foremost Israelite soldier at the time. He came immediately from his home in Kedesh.

Deborah said to Barak, "The Lord, the God of Israel, commands you: 'Go, take with you ten thousand men of Naphtali and Zebulun, and lead the way to Mount Tabor. I will lure Sisera, the commander of Jabin's army, with his chariots and his troops to the Kishon River and give him into your hands" (Judges 4:6-7 NIV).

Deborah was very specific and direct, designating a meeting place, what tribes to summon, and how many men to select. She was confident God would give them victory.

Barak surely must have been astounded by the boldness of Deborah's God-given plan. Notice that he said to her, "If you go with me, I will go; but if you don't go with me, I won't go" (Judges 4:8 NIV).

Did he need her courage? Perhaps he was in agreement with fighting the Canaanites but lacked the confidence and felt the need to have some of Deborah's confidence rub off on him. Or did he think situations would come up where he would need her on-the-spot advice and counsel? Or was he testing her faith? Was what she was asking of him so preposterous—their puny army going up against 900 iron chariots—that he wanted to see how strongly she believed what she was saying? As we would say in our culture, "Put your money where your mouth is," he was saying, "If you are so sure God is going to give us victory, then go with me. If you are so confident God is going to rescue us, then let's see you encounter the dangers of war."

Whatever his reason, Deborah didn't hesitate about going. She wasn't afraid of Sisera, his huge army or his 900 chariots, but she added a twist that Barak probably wasn't expecting. She said to him, "I will go with you, but because of the way you are going about this, the honor will not be yours, for the Lord will hand Sisera over to a woman" (Judges 4:9 NIV).

What did Deborah mean? Was she going to get the credit? Or was another woman going to be a part of the picture? The answer didn't seem to matter to Barak; what he needed and wanted was for Deborah to go with him.

Off to battle

"Deborah arose, and went with Barak to Kedesh" (Judges 4:9 KJV). In *All the Women of the Bible*, Elizabeth Deen wrote, "That one word 'arose' best explains her positive action. She did not sit at home and ponder the matter when the time came for action, but she arose, believing firmly that she was armed with strength from God."[1]

At Kedesh, Barak rallied the Israelite tribes of Zebulun and Napthtali. Just as Deborah prophesied, 10,000 men responded and followed them to the battlefield.

Meanwhile, as word spread that thousands of Israelites were ready to fight the Canaanites, others geared up for the action. Sisera gathered together his men and their 900 iron chariots and headed for the plains. Although the chariots were mighty and wicked, they needed level ground to operate.

Heber, a Kenite, left other Kenites to camp with his clan near the battlefield. The Kenites were the descendants of Hodab, Moses' brother-in-law, and usually pro-Israeli, but for some reason, Heber decided to side with the Canaanites. Maybe it was because Jabin's army seemed to have the military advantage and he wanted to be on the winner's side.

Not having chariots, Deborah and Barak and their troops headed for the hills surrounding the plains. On Mount Tabor, they could look out and see Sisera's massive armies and the many chariots. What an intimidating sight! Barak and the troops may have hesitated at this point because Deborah had to be decisive to get the men to move. She exclaimed, "Go! This is the day the Lord has given Sisera into your hands. Has not the Lord gone ahead of you?" (Judges 4:14 NIV).

Her command to "Go!" and her reminder that God was in charge was what the troops needed, and they charged down the mountain. What confidence Deborah exercised! She knew God would rescue them, and he did in a way none of them would have predicted.

The mountains melted

As the Israelite troops moved towards the Canaanites, God unleashed a sudden heavy rain. "The earth trembled, and the heavens dropped, the clouds also dropped water. The mountains melted" (Judges 5:4-5 KJV). The heavy rain pelted Sisera, his men, and his charioteers. So violent was the rain that the heavy iron chariots sank deep in the mud.

This unanticipated development caused the Canaanite troops to panic. They abandoned the chariots and started running. The Israelite soldiers were energized, and they killed the Canaanite chariot drivers and other soldiers. In the ensuing chaos, Sisera abandoned his chariot and fled. He ran for his life through the blinding rain and managed to reach the area where Heber's clan was camping.

Because there were friendly relations between King Jabin and Heber's clan, Sisera thought that he would be safe in their camp, but not everyone in the camp was sympathetic to Sisera's cause. Heber's wife Jael, whom we'll learn more about in chapter 10 of this book, offered Sisera hospitality. Trusting her, he relaxed and fell asleep in her tent. She seized the opportunity and killed him. When Barak came by looking for Sisera, Jael said, "The man you are looking for is in my tent." Just as Deborah had prophesied, the mighty Sisera was brought down by a woman. The battle was over.

Barak and Deborah were exuberant after the Israelite victory and broke into song. They couldn't help themselves; they just had to express themselves. Joining their voices together, they rejoiced that their people were no longer enslaved.

The victory song

In their song, Deborah and Barak credited God for the victory. He was the one who had caused the earth to tremble, torrents of rain to drop, and the mountains to melt.

They also acknowledged the tribes of Israel who responded to Barak's call for help. They were praised, and those who didn't help were chastised. And they also praised Jael for putting Sisera to death.

Deborah did not applaud herself nor take credit for the victory, but she did reveal an interesting detail about her nature in the song. When things were at the worst, when the inhabitants of the villages ceased, she said, "I arose a mother in Israel" (Judges 5:7 KJV). With her kind of prowess, she could have referred to herself as a mighty warrior, or if she had been familiar with such terms, as a superhero or a *Wonder* Woman—but instead she referred to herself as a mother to the Israelites. Do mothers fight? You bet they do, when their children are in trouble. Deborah had the kind of hovering, caring concern of a mother who recognizes children in trouble, tries to pump confidence in them, and does courageous things to help them.

Throughout the song, one senses Deborah's extreme devotion to God, her concern for the well-being of her nation, and her sensitivity for others. She was even sensitive to a mother in the enemy camp. Even though she was overjoyed at the victory that included Sisera's death, she couldn't help but think about his mother. In a vivid word picture (Judges 5:28–30), she voiced what the situation must be like at the moment for Sisera's mother. She would be waiting for her son to come home; she would be wondering why he was late and what was taking him so long. While the mother of Israel was happy, she was aware of the sorrow that another mother would soon experience.

Deborah stood out in times of lawlessness and disorganization. She had a willingness to trust God that was in stark contrast to the fearful, unfaithful people of the nation of Israel. She had so many roles and was so capable that today's women might be intimidated by her instead of inspired. They might hesitate to throw their lassos in her direction, but I would encourage them to reconsider.

To identify with a person doesn't mean that you have to be like her in every way. It does mean that there's a link between you—a link that will help you be a better person or inspire you to take action. For example, Deborah was braver than I'll ever be. You won't find me going up against 900 iron chariots, but still she has helped me. She's been there for me, shining light on my question, Can you be a strong woman and serve the Lord? She was there when I needed her.

When I needed Deborah

The pastor of a little church my husband and I were members of shocked us one Sunday morning by resigning. None of us had a clue it was coming. I quickly assessed the situation and realized what an impact this was going to have. We hadn't been a church very long, and David (not his real name) had been our pastor from the beginning when we were a mission. Since this group had not experienced the transition of losing their leader and finding another one, I knew we needed to act quickly and make plans or we would lose our momentum and possibly even disintegrate.

After the service, I asked another couple to join us for lunch so we could talk about the future. By initiating this little gathering, I had no intention of bypassing the governmental structure of the church. Rather I just wanted to explore some possibilities on how we could handle this crisis and keep the little church going.

Over soup and sandwiches, we sketched out some ideas and prayed. Later I asked Pastor David to let us have the Wednesday evening service time to discuss with the members in his presence various approaches and address the concerns of the people. He thought it was a good idea and agreed to meet with us.

I asked Bob, my husband, to call the director of the region our church was a part of and ask him to meet with us. Since we were a fledgling group, I thought we needed him present to know what was going on in case we would need his help in the future.

At the meeting, everyone participated. Pastor David listed for us all of his responsibilities and then we worked on finding a church member to cover each of those responsibilities. When no one volunteered to be church moderator, I said, "I will be glad to do it."

The associational director said, "You would be a good one. You're bossy."

Now I'll admit he wasn't the first person who has ever called me bossy, but his words caught me off guard.

I immediately retreated from the dialogue, although no one seemed to notice! Nor did anyone else volunteer to be the moderator!

After we got home, Bob said, "You know, he would never have said that to a man. He would have been glad for a 'take charge' person to hover over this fragile congregation."

And maybe because I was hurt, I said, "Just think, he wouldn't even have been at the meeting if I hadn't thought of inviting him."

For several days, I thought about quitting to avoid being labeled "bossy." But I didn't because I had a Deborah flame burning within me. What was hanging in the balance at our little church didn't begin to compare to what the Israelites were up against with the Canaanites, but there was something in Deborah's spirit and stance that spoke to me. As Deborah was a mother in Israel, I could be a mother in a little church until we found a new pastor. I had the time to do it; I worked part-time when most all of the other members worked full-time. More importantly, I had a vision and a love for our little church. I could be a hovering mother who could help this little congregation along until we found a new pastor. And yes, I was forceful and direct; this meant I could say, "Let's go. Let's work together because the Lord is going to deliver us!"

Her willingness to command the troops and to face 900 chariots and a powerful army puts Deborah in the *wonder* woman category. But it is her visionary concern for her people and her strong personality that makes me lasso her and find courage for my own life. Deborah taught me—and continues to teach me—that you can be a strong woman and serve the Lord.

Becoming a *wonder* woman

How do you feel about bold, articulate, and direct women? How do the members of your church or small group feel?

Can a woman be bold, direct, assertive, and articulate within the Christian community and still be liked?

Sometimes! depends on location - circumstance

How many different roles did Deborah have? What do you think her various roles contributed to her wisdom?

Why do you think Barak wanted Deborah to go into battle with him? What does Deborah's readiness to go to battle say about her? She was a fighter

What trait puts Deborah in the "*wonder* woman, able to leap over tall buildings in a single bound" category?

What interesting detail did Deborah reveal about herself in the victory song she and Barak sang? How could having this trait help a strong woman serve the Lord?

"Mother" to Israel

Chapter Three

ESTHER

Undaunted by Death to Save Her People

Wanting to add interest to a talk I was preparing, I thought about dressing as Wonder Woman. In my mind's eye, I pictured unbuttoning my cardigan at the end of my talk, revealing a shirt with a Wonder Woman insignia underneath. I had in mind a yellow, blue, and red shirt similar to Superman's. Not having read Wonder Woman comics when I was a girl nor having watched her very much on TV, I had only a vague idea of the kind of outfit Wonder Woman wore.

Wanting more information, I researched her on the Internet and saw what she looked like. Whoops, I thought, I don't think I'll be portraying Wonder Woman. I don't have the figure or the face to be Wonder Woman Lynda Carter-style—never have, never will—so you may wonder why a beauty queen is on my *wonder* women list. If I had trouble identifying with Rahab, a prostitute, how could I relate to a beauty queen? I can relate because there is more to Esther than meets the eye.

Winning the beauty contest

Esther was an orphaned Jew who lived hundreds of years after Rahab and Deborah. She did not live in the Promised Land; she lived in Persia and was cared for by her cousin Mordecai after her parents died. While she was a "beautiful young woman, and had a good figure" (Esther 2:7 GNT), she might not have been catapulted to fame if it hadn't been for a beauty contest.

King Ahasuerus, also known as King Xerxes, ruled the Persian provinces. King Ahasuerus loved battles, women, and parties, and he didn't always think through his decisions. One decision he regretted making was banishing his wife, Queen Vashti. As he brooded over his loss, his advisors suggested a beauty contest to find young women to add to his harem. "We can have agents throughout the empire to select beautiful young women for your harem. The one who pleases you the most can take Vashti's place."

When news of the contest became public, many young, beautiful women were gathered at the palace. The contestants were placed in the care of Hegai, the eunuch in charge of the king's harem. Hegai liked Esther. She won his favor and "the favor of everyone who saw her" (Esther 2:15d NIV). She definitely would have won the Miss Congeniality title even if she hadn't won the beauty contest!

Because Hegai favored her, he lost no time in beginning her beauty treatment of massages and special diets. The sole purpose of the women in the harem was to serve the king and to await his call for sexual pleasure; a pleasing body, in Hegai's thinking, was important.

Esther was compliant. She listened to the advice of Hegai and Mordecai. Mordecai told her to not tell anyone she was Jewish because they were exiles from Judea. Years earlier, the Jews had been taken away from their homeland and even though they had adapted well to living in Persia, from time to time prejudice erupted against the foreign ethnic group in the Persians' midst.

Like most parents when they first let their children go, Mordecai was anxious about Esther's welfare. "Every day Mordecai would walk back and forth in front of the courtyard of the harem, in order to find out how she was getting along and what was going to happen to her" (Esther 2:11 GNT). He needn't have worried because she won Ahasuerus's heart and with it the contest. The king gave Esther a royal crown and made her queen.

Mordecai was an observant, honest man. As he hung out around the palace, making sure Esther was OK, he learned that two palace guards were angry at the king and were plotting to kill him. Mordecai passed on the information to Queen Esther, who told the king. An investigation was made, the two men were found guilty, and punished. Mordecai's efforts saved the king's life, and this deed was recorded in the official record books.

Mordecai was also a man of integrity who couldn't bring himself to bow down to Haman, the newly appointed prime minister, the person second-in-command to King Ahasuerus. As a Jew he may have felt that bowing in homage to another human was a form of idolatry and that kind of homage belonged to God only. Whatever Mordecai's reason, his refusal resulted in big trouble for God's people.

Mordecai asks Esther to help

Haman, enjoying the power of his new position, was enraged

when Mordecai did not give the expected reverential bow. All the king's servants bowed in Haman's presence, but Mordecai refused to do so. For this irreverence, Haman hated Mordecai. As he fumed and stewed about it, he knew he wanted to get rid of Mordecai, and the more he fumed, the more he realized he wanted to get rid of all the Jews in the empire.

To accomplish this, he asked King Ahasuerus to sign a law stating that all Jews would be put to death on a certain day. He didn't tell Ahasuerus who the people were that needed to be exterminated, and Ahasuerus didn't ask!

Haman simply called them "a certain people dispersed and scattered among the peoples in all the provinces of your kingdom" (Esther 3:8 NIV). He said that their "customs are different from those of all other people" and they "do not obey the king's laws; it is not in the king's best interest to tolerate them. If it pleases the king, let a decree be issued to destroy them" (Esther 3:8–9 NIV).

A decree was granted and issued. "Dispatches were sent by couriers to all the king's provinces with the order to destroy, kill and annihilate all the Jews—young and old, women and little children—on a single day—the thirteenth day of the twelfth month, the month of Adar, and to plunder their goods" (Esther 3:13 NIV).

Esther, in her cocooned environment, did not hear about this decree, and no one thought to tell her because no one knew she was Jewish. But Mordecai heard and so did the other Jews. "In every province to which the edict and order of the king came, there was great mourning among the Jews, with fasting, weeping and wailing. Many lay in sackcloth and ashes" (Esther 4:3 NIV). Mordecai sat near the palace gate in sackcloth and ashes, wailing loudly and bitterly about the decree.

Some of the harem eunuchs and Esther's maids saw Mordecai and told her. She sent clothes for him to put on instead of his sackcloth, but he would not accept them. Esther couldn't figure out what was going on; this was so unlike Mordecai. She sent Hathach, one of the king's eunuchs, to find out what was troubling Mordecai.

When Hathach went out to him, Mordecai told him about the edict for the annihilation of the Jews. He gave Hathach a copy of the text so he could show Esther and explain it to her. He told the eunuch, "Please urge Esther to go into the king's presence to beg for mercy and plead with him for her people."

"Hathach did this, and Esther gave him this message to take back to Mordecai: 'If anyone, man or woman, goes to the inner courtyard and sees the king without being summoned, that person must die. That is the law; everyone, from the king's advisers to the people in the provinces, knows that. There is only one way to get round this law: if the king holds out his gold scepter to someone, then that person's life is spared. But it has been a month since the king sent for me'" (Esther 4:9-11 GNT).

"When Hathach told Mordecai what Esther had said, Mordecai sent her this message: 'Don't think that just because you live in the king's house you're the one Jew who will get out of this alive. If you persist in staying silent at a time like this, help and deliverance will arrive for the Jews from someplace else; but you and your family will be wiped out. Who knows? *Maybe you were made queen for just such a time as this*.'" (Esther 4:12–14 NIV; author's italics).

Mordecai's words were sobering words, challenging words. She realized he was right. She agreed to approach King Ahasuerus, even if she died trying. She would need support to do it. "Then Esther sent this reply to Mordecai: 'Go, gather together all the Jews who are in Susa [the capital city], and fast for me. Do not eat or drink for three days, night or day. I and my maids will fast as you do. When this is done, I will go to the king, even though it is against the law. *If I perish, I perish*'" (Esther 4:15-16 NIV; author's italics).

Mordecai did everything that Esther told him to do. For three days the people spiritually prepared themselves for the crucial moment when Esther would go before the king.

When the time came

On the third day of her fast, Esther dressed up "and stood in the inner courtyard of the palace, facing the throne room. The king was inside, seated on the royal throne, facing the entrance" (Esther 5:1 GNT).

"When the king saw Queen Esther standing outside, she won his favor, and he held out to her the gold scepter. She then came up and touched the tip of it" (Esther 5:2 GNT).

"'What is it, Queen Esther?' the king asked. 'Tell me what you want, and you shall have it—even if it is half my empire'" (Esther 5:3 GNT).

With this kind of encouragement, Esther could have just blurted out what she wanted, but she didn't.

She invited King Ahasuerus to a banquet that night and asked him to bring Haman with him. "Over the wine the king asked her, 'Tell me what you want, and you shall have it. I will grant your request, even if you ask for half my empire'" (Esther 5:6 GNT).

Again she did not tell him what she wanted. Why didn't she get on with it? Was she hesitating out of fear of revealing who she was or did she fear some kind of reprisal from Haman? Or was it a psychological ploy, holding off and building suspense so the king would be more receptive when she finally told him what she wanted?

"Esther replied, 'If Your Majesty is kind enough to grant my request, I would like you and Haman to be my guests tomorrow at another banquet that I will prepare for you. At that time I will tell you want I want'" (Esther 5:7-8 GNT).

After the party

Haman must have felt very special to be included in this small banquet. When he left, he was feeling "happy and in a good mood" (Esther 5:9 GNT). But on the way home his mood changed when Mordecai did not rise or show respect as Haman passed. This lack of acknowledgment made him furious as usual, but he controlled himself until he got home.

Once home, he boasted to his friends and wife about how rich he was and how pleased he was to be in the king's favor, but he admitted, he was still bugged by Mordecai's treatment of him. His listeners fanned the flames of his hatred.

They said, "Why don't you have a gallows built, seventy-five feet tall? Tomorrow morning you can ask the king to have Mordecai hanged on it, and then you can go to the banquet happy" (Esther 5:14 GNT). Oh my, if they and he only knew that Esther was Mordecai's cousin and that he was her beloved guardian!

Haman hummed as he planned the gallows. Clearly, he thought his career was about to reach new heights, and now with the gallows, he would be free of Mordecai. Life was going to be good.

While he slept well that night, the king didn't. God "blessed" the king with insomnia. While he was awake, he decided to have the official records read to him. What he heard changed everything.

King Ahasuerus read how Mordecai had uncovered a plot that had saved his life. The king asked his servants, "How have we honored and rewarded Mordecai for this?"

"His servants answered, 'Nothing has been done for him'" (Esther 6:3 GNT).

The king decided to honor Mordecai for saving his life so when Haman arrived early to work that morning, he asked him, "What should be done for someone I want to honor?"

Haman beamed because he knew the king meant him so he said, "The honoree should be placed on the king's horse and led through town by a high official."

The king said, "I want to honor Mordecai in this way. Would you take care of it?"

After the humiliating deed was done, Haman "hurried home, covering his face in embarrassment." His wife and friends told him what he knew in the pit of his stomach, "You are beginning to lose power to Mordecai. He is a Jew, and you cannot overcome him" (Esther 6:12–13 GNT). While they were talking, the palace eunuchs arrived to take Haman to Esther's banquet.

At the banquet, the king asked Esther again what she wanted. This time she explained everything. She said, "My wish is that I may live and that my people may live. My people and I have been sold for slaughter. If it were nothing more serious than being sold into slavery, I would have kept quiet and not bothered you about it; but we are about to be destroyed—exterminated!" (Esther 7:3–4 GNT).

King Ahasuerus was aghast at the news. "How could such a thing be? Who would dare do such a thing?"

Esther pointed her finger at Haman.

Enraged at how he had been set up by Haman to destroy all these people, the king left the room to deal with his feelings. Once again he had made an unwise decision.

Quickly surveying the situation, Haman figured the king would punish him for "this, so he stayed behind to beg Queen Esther for his life. He had just thrown himself down on Esther's couch to beg for mercy, when the king came back into the room from the gardens" (Esther 7:7–8 GNT).

When the king saw Haman in this position, he thought he was trying to rape Esther. He was totally repulsed and disgusted. He asked Harbonah, a eunuch, for advice. He suggested they hang Haman on the gallows meant for Mordecai. The king agreed, so the archenemy of the Jews met his just fate, but the Jews still weren't safe from extermination. Once a Persian proclamation had been issued in the king's name and stamped with the royal seal, it could not be revoked. It was still on the books that on a specified day, all Jews would be killed.

Israel's deliverance

King Ahasuerus gave Queen Esther Haman's estate and knowing now that Mordecai was Esther's cousin and adopted father, he "took off his ring—which he had taken back from Haman—and gave it to Mordecai [appointing him Prime Minister]; and Esther appointed Mordecai to be in charge of Haman's estate" (Esther 8:2 TLB).

As rewarding as this must have been to both Esther and Mordecai, God's people still weren't safe from extermination. The decree was still in effect—on that appointed day, the Jews would be killed. A proclamation issued in the king's name and stamped with the royal seal could not be revoked.

So once more, Esther approached the king. She fell down at his feet and begged him with tears to stop the extermination of the Jews. She said, "If it please Your Majesty, and if you love me, send out a decree reversing Haman's order to destroy the Jews throughout the king's provinces. For how can I endure it, to see my people butchered and destroyed?" (Esther 8:5–6 TLB).

While Persian laws could not be repealed, they could be offset by another law; therefore, King Ahasuerus gave permission to Mordecai to issue a degree that would offset the first one without actually canceling it. Mordecai's decree let the Jews defend themselves on the day they were to have been killed. God's people in Persia were safe once again, thanks to Esther's bravery.

We never know when we will be in a position to be a *wonder* woman like Esther. *What?* Yes, that's right. We may not be queens with the deliverance of a whole nation of people depending on us, but we all have assets that God might want us to use in a certain situation, and He might move us into positions where who we are can make a difference if we have Esther's courage.

For such a time as this

Esther's beauty was an asset but it would not have meant that much—would not have made her heroic—if she hadn't been in the position she was. If she had been lovely Esther living out somewhere in one of the far off provinces of the Persian Empire, she could not have saved the Jews, and we would have never heard of her. But through circumstances that she had no control over—circumstances that God orchestrated—she gained a position of influence.

At sometime in our lives, we may find ourselves in a similar position where our response, our rising to the occasion, our actions, could make a difference. It could be a dangerous situation, in which someone needs rescuing from a burning car or an abusive home. It could be one in which you observe dishonesty—for example, someone in your company is cheating, and employees and stockholders will lose thousands of dollars unless someone says something. It could be a ministry situation, where a need is crying out for a response—a need that you see. It could be a call to missions, where you see a field ripe unto harvest and you wonder, Why doesn't someone do something about this?

Perhaps God has placed you in a position "for such a time as this." If He has, will you have Esther's courage to respond? Now that's the trait we want to emulate. Esther's courage is what makes her a *wonder* woman.

Becoming a *wonder* woman

What were Esther's assets? What was her strongest one?

What are your assets?

What kind of spiritual help did Esther seek from the Jews before approaching the King about the edict that all Jews would perish?

How might you recognize when God has put you in a "position for such a time as this?"

What do the words "if I perish, I perish" indicate about what Esther thought she might have to do? What do they say about her attitude?

What do Rahab, Deborah, and Esther have in common? What traits do they share that put them in the category of *wonder* women "able to leap over tall buildings in a single bound?"

Part 2

ISN'T SHE WONDERFUL?

In the first part of this book, we looked at the Bible's *superstrong* women. Deborah, Rahab, and Esther were daring, courageous women who played pivotal roles in the history of God's people. They were women who were able to "leap over tall buildings in a single bound."

In Part 2 we'll look at women who are quite different from the *superstrong* women. These women are super in another way—they are *supercaring*. They are women about whom we would exclaim, "Isn't she wonderful?"

We don't ask a question like this about everyone we know.

This descriptive question is reserved for a special few—women whose generosity, caring, or kindness is out of the ordinary. When we ask, "Isn't she wonderful?" about these women, we ask it with affection. The attitude and actions of *supercaring* women stir up warm feelings inside us. We may not even be the recipients of their kindnesses or love, but our hearts are touched and inspired by their examples.

Chapter Four

RUTH

What a Daughter-in-Law!

The Old Testament Book of Ruth

As the meeting ended, some women lingered behind to discuss the presentation. While it hadn't been on love specifically, the speaker's topic generated discussion about being loved and feeling loved. After several shared their stories, Elsie spoke of being physically abused as a child by a violent father. When she married, her husband verbally abused her and mistreated her. Now she was a widow in poor health living with her son and his wife. She said, "I never knew unconditional love until Mary Rose loved me."

We all went "Wow!" Mary Rose was her daughter-in-law! Maybe we shouldn't have reacted that way but you just don't expect to hear about a daughter-in-law having unlimited, unqualified love for a mother-in-law. You usually hear about friction between them. Sometimes you even hear about them becoming good friends, but that was the first time I heard about a daughter-in-law having unconditional love for her mother-in-law. Wait a minute. Make that the second time. The first was when Ruth loved her mother-in-law, Naomi. She was so committed to Naomi that those who knew her couldn't help but say, "Isn't Ruth *wonderful*?"

How they met

Ruth was a resident of Moab, not the Promised Land where God's people lived. Her culture was different, and the god she worshiped was different from Yahweh, the God of the Israelites. The Moabites worshipped Chemosh, and this worship difference was one reason the Moabites and the Israelites disliked each other. Consequently, Ruth probably grew up never thinking of marrying an Israelite, but then she met Mahlon.

Mahlon, his brother Kilion, and his parents Naomi and Elimelech, moved from Bethlehem of Judah to Moab to escape a famine. The move was difficult and the adjustment hard, but it was necessary. It meant their family would survive, or so they thought. Then tragedy struck: Elimelech died. Perhaps sensing how fragile life is and feeling the need for more family, Mahlon and Kilion married. Mahlon married Ruth, and Kilion married Orpah.

Naomi probably had mixed feelings about her sons marrying Moabite women. She would have preferred they married Israelites, but she realized that couldn't happen with their living in Moab. She did, though, welcome the companionship of the women. She also looked forward to the time when she might have grandchildren, but year after year passed with no grandchildren being born.

After ten years, Mahlon and Kilion died, and so Naomi "was bereft of her two sons and her husband" (Ruth 1:5 AMP). She coped the best she could, but she worried about how the three would survive. In those days, a woman was almost completely dependent on the men for her welfare. This was not a time of equal employment opportunity for women or Social Security benefits for widows. In fact, a woman had few, if any, ways to provide for herself.

Naomi heard that the famine back in Bethlehem was over. She still had relatives and friends there so she decided to return home, taking her daughters-in-law with her. As they started out, Naomi remembered how hard it was for her to leave her home and move to a strange land. She also thought of the future of Ruth and Orpah. She wanted them to remarry and have children, and she knew it would be unlikely that any Israelites would want to marry them. Wanting a happy life for them, she said, "Go back, each of you, to your mother's home. May the LORD show kindness to you, as you have shown to your dead and to me. May the LORD grant that each of you will find rest in the home of another husband" (Ruth 1:8 NIV).

Then Naomi kissed them good-bye, but Orpah and Ruth would have none of it. "They wept aloud. And they said to her, 'No, we will return with you to your people'" (Ruth 1:8–10 AMP).

As heartbreaking as this moment must have been, Naomi insisted they return home. She pointed out the improbability of their ever having husbands if they came with her. How hopeless the future looked to Naomi! She cried, "The LORD's hand has gone out against me!" (Ruth 1:13 NIV).

Orpah chose to stay, and we can't fault her. Home and the familiar have a strong pull, as they should, which makes it remarkable that Ruth insisted on going with Naomi. Ruth loved Naomi so much that she clung to her. She wasn't going to let Naomi go without her, and she said so with some of the most beautiful words of commitment ever written.

Promised love

Ruth said to Naomi, "Entreat me not to leave thee, or to return from following after thee: for whither thou goest, I will go; and where thou lodgest, I will lodge: thy people shall be my people, and thy God my God: Where thou diest, will I die, and there will I be buried: the LORD do so to me, and more also, if ought but death part thee and me" (Ruth 1:16–17 KJV).

Ruth's entreaty was firm: I am going to do this; you are not going to stop me.

Ruth's entreaty was endearing. Whose heart wouldn't melt with words like the ones she spoke?

Ruth's attitude was one of determination. She was going to see this through. She would go wherever Naomi went. Wherever Naomi lived, in whatever kind of dwelling or circumstances, Ruth would be right there with her.

Naomi's people would become her people. While she knew she would probably be mistreated as a foreigner, Ruth would not mistreat the Israelites. She would adopt Naomi's kin as her own.

She even offered the most personal part of herself as a part of this love package. She would accept Naomi's faith and worship her God. She said, "Your God will be my God" (Ruth 1:16 GNT).

Ruth did not put a time limit on this commitment. She didn't say, "I'll stay with you until we get to Bethlehem." Or "I'll stay for several years and when you are good and settled, I'll return to Moab." She said, "Wherever you die, I will die, and that is where I will be buried. May the **Lord's** worst punishment come upon me if I let anything but death separate me from you!" (Ruth 1:17 GNT).

If Naomi died first, Ruth would stay and be buried in her land. She wouldn't return to Moab even then. What she was really saying was, "You can trust me. I'm going to be there for you, through the thick and thin, through the good times and bad." She was making a lifetime commitment.

But as beautiful and as meaningful as the words were, as far-reaching as they were, they still had to be tested to show genuine commitment. Ruth's words convinced Naomi that she was determined to go, but what would happen once Ruth and Naomi were back in Bethlehem? Would Ruth be true to her promise when she faced the adjustment of a new culture and dealt with challenging circumstances?

Living the love she promised

Ruth might have encountered the first test of her commitment when the two women arrived back in Bethlehem. Sadness engulfed Naomi as she was painfully reminded of her losses and what her life used to be like. When her old friends and acquaintances saw her, they were excited. They said, "Is this really Naomi?"

"Don't call me Naomi," she told them. "Call me Mara, because the Almighty has made my life very bitter. I went away full, but the LORD has brought me back empty. Why call me Naomi? The LORD has afflicted me; the Almighty has brought misfortune upon me" (Ruth 1:20–21 NIV).

As Ruth heard Naomi's complaints, she might have been tempted to think, Naomi did not come back empty. She has me. Where is her confidence in the Lord that she encouraged me to believe in? Have I made a mistake to leave Moab? But Ruth didn't respond like that; she was true to her commitment. She stayed with her even though Naomi was depressed and the two were destitute.

Fortunately, it was harvest time. When Ruth heard that foreigners and widows could glean grain dropped by harvesters in the fields, she went looking for a field where she would be allowed to work. The Israelite law allowed for this practice, but some land owners disregarded it. While gleaning wouldn't be a long-term solution for her and Naomi, it would get them by, so she went looking for a field where the owner would be receptive to gleaners.

"So Ruth went out to the fields and walked behind the workers picking up the heads of grain which they left. It *so happened* that she was in a field that belonged to Boaz" (Ruth 2:3 GNT; author's italics). Boaz was a rich and influential man who was a relative of Elimelech's.

What might have seemed happenstance to Ruth was God's way of responding to her committed love and her trust in Him. God used His happenstance to bring two people together—two people who would make three people happy.

Under His wings

As Ruth moved through the field picking up grain, Boaz noticed her. He asked his foreman, "Who's that girl?"

The foreman replied, "It's that girl from Moab—you know, the one who came back with Naomi. She asked me this morning if she could pick up the grains dropped by the reapers, and she has been at it ever since. What a hard worker!"

Boaz went over and talked to her. He called her "child" as older adults often call younger ones. "Listen, my child," he said. "Stay right here with us to glean; don't think of going to any other fields. Stay right behind my women workers; I have warned the young men not to bother you: when you are thirsty, go and help yourself to the water" (Ruth 2:8–9 TLB).

Ruth realized he was being unusually considerate of a foreigner and thanked him warmly. She asked, "How can you be so kind to me?"

Boaz said, "I also know about all the love and kindness you have shown your mother-in-law since the death of your husband, and how you left your father and mother in your own land and have come here to live among strangers'" (Ruth 2:10–11 TLB). Word had spread through the community as people recognized how *wonder*ful Ruth was.

Marveling at her loving kindness, Boaz wished to see her blessed. He said, "May the LORD repay you for what you have done. May you be richly rewarded by the LORD, the God of Israel, under whose wings you have come to take refuge" (Ruth 2:12 NIV).

When Ruth went back to the field, it wasn't difficult to find grain because Boaz told his harvesters to protect Ruth and leave extra grain for her.

When she had beaten out what she had gleaned, she had nearly a bushel. She took the grain home and showed Naomi. Naomi was amazed. "Where in the world did you glean today? Whose field have you been working in?"

Ruth told Naomi about gleaning in Boaz's field and about his being kind to her.

"'Praise the Lord for a man like that! God has continued his kindness to us as well as to your dead husband!' Naomi cried excitedly. 'Why, that man is one of our closest relatives!'" (Ruth 2:20 TLB).

Notice how Naomi's mood had changed. She was no longer pessimistic. Her mental wheels were turning as she thought about this man; since he was a relative, he might be the solution to their problems. Her hopes rose considerably.

Ruth said, "He said to come back and stay close behind his reapers until the entire field is harvested" (Ruth 2:21 TLB).

"'This is wonderful!' Naomi exclaimed. 'Do as he has said. Stay with his girls right through the whole harvest; you will be safer there than in any other field!'" (Ruth 2:22 TLB).

Ruth could have bristled at these instructions and testily responded, "That's exactly what I was planning to do." Often a point of tension between older adults and younger adults is this matter of "giving" advice. The older ones see it as sharing wisdom while the younger ones think, Can't she see I can think for myself? She treats me like a child.

But Ruth didn't respond to Naomi's instructions like that. She was compliant, but these instructions were reasonable. What would happen if Naomi suggested something unreasonable? Would she be compliant then?

You've got to be kidding!

As the harvesting of barley and then wheat continued, Ruth kept gleaning and Naomi did some serious thinking. The hope of an Israelite widow was that the nearest of kin to her dead husband would take her as his wife. Mosaic Law said that if a widow had no son but could still bear children, the deceased husband's brother was supposed to produce a son with her (see Deuteronomy 25:5–10). If they had a son, that son would take the name of the former husband and the dead man's family would continue. This law wouldn't help in Ruth's case as her brother-in-law was dead, but the sense of relative helping relative was inherent in this law.

Another practice among God's people that Naomi thought of was the redemption of land which might be lost from a husbandless family because of heavy debt or some other fate. The law called for a kinsman-redeemer to step up and redeem the family name and property of a deceased relative.

Since Boaz was a relative, maybe he could be their *kinsman-redeemer*. The idea occurred to Naomi, but it hadn't occurred to Boaz. How could she get him to see the possibility of marrying Ruth and redeeming their family situation? How could she get him to do what she wanted?

Because he was a cousin and not a brother and because he was older than Ruth, Boaz might never see himself as marrying Ruth. He needed some "encouragement" to see what Naomi was seeing.

Naomi knew that when the harvest ended, there would be much celebration and drinking. She also knew the owners of the fields would sleep near the harvested grain to keep it from being stolen.

Naomi told Ruth to bathe, put on perfume, and dress in her best clothes. She told her to sneak down to the threshing floor where Boaz was spending the night. Once he had eaten, had plenty of wine, and fallen asleep, Ruth must uncover his feet and lie next to him until he noticed her.

It would have been at this point that I would have said, "You've got to be kidding!" This plan was fraught with danger. What if someone such as a man bent on stealing grain saw her moving in the darkness and harmed her? What if Boaz were frightened by the unexpected presence of a person when he awakened out of a deep sleep? People aren't always rational when groggy. Might he attack her? What if he didn't recognize who she was and forced himself on her? Or what would Boaz think of her showing up in the night like this? What kind of woman would he think her to be?

There were plenty of reasons to reject Naomi's plan, but Ruth didn't. She dressed as her mother-in-law said and went to the threshing floor. What a daughter-in-law! Fortunately, Naomi's plan worked.

Will you marry me?

When Boaz discovered someone at his feet in the darkness, Boaz asked, "Who are you?"

"I am your servant Ruth," she said. "Spread the corner of your garment over me, since you are a kinsman-redeemer" (Ruth 3:9 NIV). If she was going to be under the wings of God as Boaz had prayed, then she needed to be under Boaz' wing, thus the reference to spreading his garment, his protective covering, over her.

Boaz was moved by her request. He said, "This kindness is greater than that which you showed earlier: You have not run after the younger men, whether rich or poor. And now, my daughter, don't be afraid. I will do for you all you ask. All my fellow townsmen know that you are a woman of noble character" (Ruth 3:10b–11 NIV). He did not hold any suspicion of ulterior motives on her part, because the townspeople all talked with admiration about her character. They said, "Isn't she *wonder*ful?"

Naomi's plan worked. Boaz found Ruth's proposal to his liking, but he was aware that someone else was nearer of kin. He informed Ruth and assured her that he would solve the problem, which he did, and Boaz and Ruth soon married.

They had a baby son and allowed him to fill the arms of Naomi. Life for her now was full, and she was again pleasant.

Naomi's friends saw how valuable Ruth was to her. When there was no one else, Ruth was there for Naomi. When Ruth could have graciously bowed out of their relationship, she didn't; instead, she committed herself to Naomi and followed her to Bethlehem to live, not just temporarily but for as long as they lived. When Naomi was bitter, Ruth was not deterred. When they needed a way to provide for themselves, Ruth went to the fields to glean. When Naomi devised a plan, Ruth did exactly as she was told and solved their survival problems.

And when Ruth had a baby boy, giving Naomi a grandchild, the friends couldn't restrain their praise. "Isn't Ruth *wonderful*?" Well, they didn't exactly use those words. Instead, they said, "Your daughter-in-law loves you, and has done more for you than seven sons" (Ruth 4:15 GNT).

Their words suggest how important having a son was to a woman of Israel. Naomi had known the loss of sons, but God made up for that through Ruth. She was worth seven sons! That was about as high a rating as one could receive, since the Israelites thought of seven as the perfect number.

The women recognized all Ruth had done for Naomi and how she had contributed to her life. They marveled at Ruth's committed love, and I do, too, which is why she's an inspiration to me. Because of Ruth's example, I want to be more loving.

Ruth's story gives me a picture of what committed love looks like. Her story reminds me of the importance of the long haul. In these days of easy come, easy go, easy in, and easy out, Ruth's example shows us consistent love, a staying love, one with no exits.

Our goal in emulating her should never be that people will call us *wonderful*. Ruth never had that goal. Her commitment was born out of genuine love. If someone would say about us, "Isn't she *wonderful*?" that might mean, we're being committed lovers, and wouldn't that be nice?

Becoming a *wonder* woman

What did Ruth give up to make her commitment to Naomi?

Commitment like Ruth's is not necessary for all relationships. What relationships call for love like Ruth's?

How important was Ruth's verbal commitment to keeping her commitment? Of what good is verbalizing commitment? Are words always needed?

If you would write down your commitment to Jesus Christ, what would you say?

Does the fact that Ruth was compliant to Naomi's instructions mean we always have to be compliant to those we love?

Chapter Five

DORCAS

Abounding in Good Works

Acts 9:36–42

Just as Boaz, the townspeople, and Naomi's neighbors said of Ruth, "Isn't she *wonderful?*" hundreds of years later, the men and women of Joppa spoke of Dorcas in the same affectionate way. By this time, after Jesus's death and resurrection, the church was developing and expanding. Signs and wonders accompanied the expansion, and Dorcas was at center stage of one of them. After getting sick and dying, she came back to life when the apostle Peter prayed for her. A pretty phenomenal event, wouldn't you agree? Luke thought so when he wrote the Book of Acts; he saw her healing as helping to spread the gospel. But her resurrection is not why people called her *wonderful*. It was who she was and what she did among them before she died. We can only imagine what they said after her resurrection!

Who was Dorcas?

Dorcas was a Christ follower who lived in Joppa, on the seacoast of Palestine (once known as the Promised Land). She was also known as Tabitha, an Aramaic name. Dorcas was her Greek name; the fact that she went by both names probably meant she mingled freely among the Jews who spoke Aramaic and among the wider Greek-speaking community.

She was part of an established group of believers that probably formed when the persecution of Christians started occurring in Jerusalem. After Jesus's resurrection and the coming of the Holy Spirit, believers fellowshipped, studied and worshipped together in Jerusalem. As they grew numerically, Jerusalem Jews began to see Christians as a threat to their faith. Persecution resulted, and consequently many believers fled, fanning out into Judea and Samaria. Some ended up at the towns of Lydda and Joppa, where they witnessed to those living there, and churches were formed.

Dorcas was a part of the Joppa church. Within her church—and perhaps within the community—she had a reputation for doing charitable works. She was "full of good works and almsdeeds" (Acts 9:36 KJV). Skilled as a seamstress, Dorcas quite likely applied those skills to sewing coats and garments for those in need.

She was a vital part of the Christian community—setting a good example, extending love, encouraging the downhearted and offering practical help, and when she suddenly became ill and died, the believers were grieved at their loss. They just hadn't expected it. And what would they do without her? Dorcas, their Dorcas? She couldn't be dead. They wrung their hands and cried because there didn't seem there was anything they could do, and they wanted to so much. Then they heard that Peter was nearby. Someone said he had healed a paralyzed man in Lydda, about ten to fifteen miles northwest of them. The community sent two men to Peter to seek his help.

Please help us, Peter!

The apostles didn't flee Jerusalem when the other believers did, but from time to time they left to visit the new congregations. That's why Peter was in Lydda. While he was there, he met a paralyzed man named Aeneas, who had not been able to get out of bed for eight years. "Aeneas," Peter said to him, "Jesus Christ makes you well. Get up and make your bed" (Acts 9:34 GNT). Immediately, Aeneas got up.

The Joppa church thought that if Peter could heal a man who had been bedfast for eight years, then maybe he could bring Dorcas back to life, particularly if he arrived quickly, while she was still close to life.

When they found Peter, they told him about Dorcas, how much she meant to them, and how they couldn't stand to lose her. They said, "Please come at once!" (Acts 9:38 NIV).

Peter hurried back with the two men. By this time, the dead body had been washed and laid out in an upstairs room. When Peter entered the room, he found the widows gathered around the body, grieving over their loss. They crowded around Peter, expressing their grief to him and "showing him all the shirts and coats that Dorcas had made while she was alive" (Acts 9:39 GNT).

The commotion and emotion in the room was too much for Peter. He needed to concentrate if he, through Christ's power, was to deliver this woman from the grip of death. Once they were out, he knelt down and prayed. In the name of Jesus, he asked God Almighty to return life to the body. Then fully expecting that his prayer was being answered, he turned to the dead body. He said, "Tabitha, get up!" She opened her eyes, and as they focused, she saw Peter and sat up.

"Peter reached over and helped her get up." She was awake, she could see, she could move, she was alive! Peter then "called all the believers, including the widows, and presented her alive to them (Acts 9:41 GNT). What a great day for the church at Joppa! Their valued member was restored to them, and they also witnessed an awesome miracle. Their happiness could not be contained so "the news about this spread all over Joppa, and many people believed in the Lord" (Acts 9:42 GNT).

Because of the unusual nature of this event, we can understand Luke's including it to show how the church developed. He doesn't, however, tell us much about Dorcas, the person. Her story is told in a few short Bible verses, so how could I conclude that people thought she was *wonder*ful?

Here's how

As I studied Acts 9:36-43, I noted three things that reveal the high regard the local Christian community had for Dorcas:

1. She was called a disciple. "In Joppa there was a *disciple* named Tabitha . . . who was always doing good and helping the poor" (Acts 9:36 NIV; author's italics). This is the first and only time in the New Testament that *disciple* is used to describe a woman.

   In a general sense, all earnest believers are disciples.

The word *disciple* means learner, pupil, or follower. In the New Testament, though, the word was also used as a label for followers of Jesus—*male* followers who surrounded Him or who were sent out by Him. Sometimes the label *disciples* was used to describe a large circle of followers. Sometimes members of a small circle such as the twelve apostles were also called disciples. Dorcas is the only woman directly referenced as a disciple.

In Acts, Luke used the term *disciple* to denote members of the Christian faith. When he learned about Dorcas as he researched his story, he discovered that she "was full of good works and charitable deeds" (Acts 9:36) as the *New King James Version* puts it, or in the words of the *New American Standard Bible*, "abounding with deeds of kindness and charity." It is not unusual for people to do good deeds—an occasional deed here and there—but a life so full of good works could only be lived by someone who, in Luke's eyes, was a disciple of Jesus. She was *wonder*ful because she was like Jesus.

2. Those in the Joppa church obviously loved Dorcas, as revealed by their urgency to get help and to get it quickly. They were well aware of the finality of death. Most people would have considered getting help for Dorcas as a waste of time since she was already dead. You can't undo death, but this group held out for the possibility that it was reversible. Their loss was so great that they just couldn't bear to let her go. They loved her so much that they sent men to Lydda who said to Peter, "Come at

once," although she was already dead.

And, too, it may have been from the Joppa church community that Luke got the title of *disciple* for Dorcas. Instead of him giving her the title, perhaps he was quoting the Joppa Christians. In the Books of Luke and Acts, Luke's many specific details show how earnest he was in getting his stories right. He wasn't always an eyewitness of what he recorded, and he wouldn't have been present for Dorcas's resurrection, because he had not yet joined a missionary journey with Paul. In the interest of accurate reporting, he simply repeated what the people he interviewed said. They saw her as doing Christ's work, and to them that made her a disciple. They meant it as a high compliment, and they said it with affection.

3. You can tell Dorcas was loved by the way "the widows" in the Joppa church responded to her death. The brief Bible passage about Dorcas seems to indicate that the widows were a specific group, one that as a whole cared a great deal about Dorcas.

    - The widows held vigil and stood by the body (Acts 9:39 NIV). When Peter arrived and was taken to the upstairs room, all the widows stood around him, "crying and showing him the robes and other clothes that Dorcas had made while she was still with them" (Acts 9:39 NIV).
    - Peter "called the saints *and* widows" (Acts 9:41 KJV; author's italics) to come see the resurrected Dorcas. It was as if the widows were a group unto themselves.

> If they were, this does not mean that the widows were not or could not be saints. Christians are called *saints* in the New Testament, a word that means "different." Christians are different from others.

One way Dorcas might have helped the widows was in making clothes for them. Maybe they were recipients of those "good works" that Dorcas abounded in. The way the widows pointed out to Peter the garments Dorcas had made suggested that they were made for them, and *The Living Bible* reads that way: "The room was filled with weeping widows who were showing one another the coats and other garments Dorcas had made for them" (Acts 9:39). Every item was a reminder to them of how precious Dorcas was and how worried they were about a future without her. Their tears and laments spoke of their affection for her.

Another way Dorcas might have helped them was by incorporating them into a group. Maybe she invited them to come to help her sew for the needy. This gave them a place to go, something to do, and people to interact with. These women who had already lost once found this fresh loss hard to take. It was as if they were losing a part of themselves so they crowded around Peter, letting him know what an unusual person she was.

As I write these reasons for my conclusion that people thought Dorcas was *wonderful*, I realize my own experiences have probably influenced my interpretation. If we're honest, that's the way it is for many of us. Our interpretation of Scripture is subjective as well as objective. Indeed, I'll readily admit that my interpretation of this passage may be influenced by my experiences starting with a very giving mother.

My generous *Mom*

I had the privilege of growing up with a mother who is like Dorcas in that she abounded in good works. She was always thinking about others and finding joy in pleasing people and making others happy. She used her cooking skills, sewing skills, craft skills and sometimes her cleaning skills to make life better or brighter for others. Because she did so much for others, many people have said of her, "Isn't she *wonder*ful?"

I did not take after my mother! And yet I did. I'm not into sewing and crafts, and I don't keep a pie in the oven most of the time. What we have to give others is different. I'm more into studying, teaching, and writing, but from her I learned the joy of giving. And every time I'm around her I'm reminded and motivated. Studying Dorcas's life does the same thing for me.

To praise Dorcas and to emulate her doesn't mean we have to abound in exactly the same things she did. There is room for a lot of variety. It wouldn't work for me to organize a sewing group when my heart is drawn toward researching and writing; but this doesn't let me off the hook, to think that I don't have to be concerned with doing the kinds of things Dorcas did. There's not much of a chance of this happening because I have some important words from childhood embedded in me that remind to me to do good works.

The Girls' Auxiliary

When Robert Fulghum's book *All I Really Need to Know I Learned in Kindergarten* came out, I thought, everything I needed to know about the Christian life I learned in Girls' Auxiliary, or "GAs," as we called it. I was a member of that missions organization for girls, and we regularly repeated the following pledge:

> Knowing that countless people grope in darkness and giving attention to his commands, I assert my allegiance to Jesus Christ, to his church and its activities, attempting with God's help to abide in Him through prayer, to advance in wisdom by Bible study, to acknowledge my stewardship of time, money, and personality, *to adorn myself* with good works, and to accept the challenge of the Great Commission.

The words stuck, and like my wedding vows ("for better, for worse"), they have replayed themselves over and over in my mind ever since. Within the pledge are five focus points to live by. We called them "Star Ideals." They certainly have been guiding lights to me through the years. One in particular reminds me that even when I am absorbed in writing and speaking, I still should be alert to opportunities to do good works. As the apostle Paul said, "As we have therefore opportunity, let us do good unto all men, especially unto them who are of the household of faith" (Galatians 6:10 KJV).

Finding ways and being kind to others softens us and adds beauty to our lives. *To adorn*, the phrase in the GA pledge, means to "make beautiful or attractive; to put ornaments on; to decorate." We become more attractive to others and so does our message about Jesus when we are kind. This may be one reason why women who *abound* in good works like Dorcas and my mother become attractive to others. People are warmed by their actions and they respond by thinking, Aren't they *wonderful*?

Women ministering to women

Another reason why I may have been influenced to interpret Dorcas's experience the way I did is because I've been on the receiving end of many acts of kindness, and I've seen the power of women ministering to others.

I have been ministered to by modern Dorcases in the many women who have made clothes for me, cared for me when I was sick, helped me with projects, brought casseroles when I had a baby, babysat my children, held my hand when I cried or prayed me through a rough spot. I know how it feels to be on the receiving end so I can understand why the people in Joppa and the widows in particular loved Dorcas and were so distraught to lose her.

I have also seen the power of women being kind and thoughtful to each other through small groups, whether they are organized for ministry, missions or even crafts. Recently, after speaking at an area church, I was visiting with a woman when another woman walked up. The second woman nodded toward the first and said, "She saved my life."

That's quite a statement. She had my interest! "Tell me about it. How did this woman save your life?"

She said, "When my husband died, I didn't want to go on living. There didn't seem to be a reason to get up in the morning, but every Tuesday and Thursday morning, this woman called. She invited me to the church's quilting group, and then she came by for me. Her calls showed me someone cared, and the quilting group gave me somewhere to go and something to do. Through that contact, I came to realize life went on and I could survive. As you can see, I have. Here I am today enjoying life."

Sounds like a Dorcas experience to me! The need goes on and on to have the rough edges of life smoothed out by women who adorn themselves with good works, women who have eyes to see needs and are willing to meet them.

Dorcas "was full of good works and charitable deeds, *which she did*" (Acts 9:36 NKJV; author's italics). How significant are the last three words! Too many well-meaning people see needs and do nothing. "They" is their favorite word, as in "Why don't *they* do something?" They sit around and talk about needs that should be met and don't lift a finger. Dorcas not only saw needs and thought of ways to relieve them, but she also carried out her plans, patterning her life after Jesus's life. No wonder she was called a *disciple!*

Dorcas's example holds possibilities for all of us. Her works were not those of a Messiah or even of a great leader, or even of a miracle worker like Peter. No, her good works were in paying attention to the needs of those around her and responding to them. She did ordinary things—ordinary things that any of us can do—and she became extraordinary. She became a *wonder* woman because she abounded in doing what any of us can do.

Becoming a *wonder* woman

How would you define "good works?"

What do you admire about people who abound in good works?

Do Christians *have to* adorn themselves with good works? Or, is this an option that doesn't have to be exercised?

When Paul instructed believers to do good, why do you think he said "especially to those who belong to the family of believers?" What difference would "good works" make in the body of Christ?

What beauty does "good works" add to a Christian's life?

Why are people who abound in good works attractive to others?

Part 3

ISN'T SHE A WONDER?

There is yet another category of *wonder* women. These are women about whom we would say, "Isn't she a wonder?" We ask this question with admiration, even awe at times, but not necessarily with the affection expressed in "Isn't she wonderful?"

Instead of posing our admiration as a question ("Isn't she a wonder?"), we might say, "I don't know how she does it." How does she keep going when she has to handle such difficult circumstances? How can she be so tenacious when the task looks impossible? How does she handle herself so well when her husband or her children disappoint her? How can she be a caregiver unendingly and never complain? How can she juggle so many roles, keep all the balls in the air and not have one hit her in the face? How can she experience so much sadness and still be joyful? We shake our heads in genuine puzzlement at *supercapable* women who have much to teach us.

Chapter Six

ANNA

You Prayed How Often?

How are you at keeping spiritual disciplines such as praying, fasting, journaling, and meditating? I work at them, even write books about some of them, but I'm always aware of how much more I could be doing. Anna is one of those people whose practice was far greater than mine and who serves as an inspiration to me. Talk about having a hero of yesterday to inspire us today—Anna inspires me.

Who was Anna?

Anna was an old woman. Although her graceful way of aging inspires me, that's not why she is my hero, although the day may come when she will be my hero for that, too. Right now, it is because of the way she handled her sorrow.

In addition to being old, Anna was a widow who lived early in the first Christian century, at the time Jesus was born. She had only been married for seven short years when her husband died, and she had lived without him a long time. She was either 84 years old or had been a widow for that same number of years. The Greek text is unclear, but either way, she had been single a long time.

She was a prophetess. Anna revealed God's will to people. Although women were excluded from the priesthood, some participated in the ministry of the Word. In the Old Testament, there was Miriam (Moses' sister), Deborah, and Huldah (advisor to King Josiah). In the New Testament, the daughters of Philip (Acts 21:9) prophesied. These women were divinely inspired to make God's will known to others.

Anna came from a notable family. She was the daughter of Phanuel of the Israeli tribe of Asher so she had a strong sense of history, one that looked forward to the coming of the Messiah.

She was a faithful, committed worshipper. The Bible says that she never left the temple in Jerusalem; she worshipped there night and day (see Luke 2:37b).

This sounds almost like an impossibility, but according to the Jewish historian Josephus, it was possible but rare.[1] The temple was divided into the Court of Gentiles, the Court of Women, the Court of Israel and the Holy Place (including the Holy of Holies). Obviously, Anna would have lived in the outermost court, called the Court of Gentiles, or in the Court of Women, beyond which women could not go. The Court of Israel was for Jewish men and the Holy Place for priests only. The whole temple complex was large with side chambers and porticoes; Matthew 24:1 refers to the "buildings" of the temple, so it was possible that Anna found a nice little alcove somewhere where she could keep a pallet and a few belongings.

Anna was adept at spiritual disciplines. She prayed and fasted day and night at the temple. She prayed for herself, she prayed for others (those who came to the temple) and she prayed for the coming of the Messiah. God's people needed a Savior.

In spite of her age (some might have considered fasting too dangerous for a woman of her advanced years), Anna kept more than the customary fasts on Mondays and Thursdays. She fasted regularly and earnestly as a means of self-sacrifice and worship.

I don't know about you, but at this point, my admiration for Anna kicks in and I think, *Isn't she a* wonder? *Isn't she a* wonder to live at the Temple, to give up her privacy, to always be available to others, to fast and to pray?

As I marvel about her God-focused ascetic lifestyle, I wonder, How did she do it? What was behind Anna's long, consistent devotion to God?

How did she do it?

The fact that Anna was single and childless may partially explain her ability to have a worship-centered lifestyle. Her life wasn't complicated by love commitments and other relationships. She could focus on God and God alone.

Living simply was also probably a big help. If she lived in the temple, her accommodations were probably very sparse. She wasn't responsible for cleaning a house. If she was fasting daily, there weren't many meals to prepare or dishes to wash. There are spiritual advantages to being single-hearted and living simply!

She was a disciplined woman. Fasting and praying as much as she did required self-discipline, especially in the early days of her widowhood. Through these practices, she was in constant communication with God, and when you talk to God, He responds! Day by day, His strength enabled her to live a simple life of worship and ministry.

Where did Anna's self-discipline come from, especially in the early days before it became habitual? Could it be that she had a heart especially attuned to spiritual things? Maybe she was motivated by a hunger and thirst for righteousness. Or perhaps she was burdened for God's people and was eager for the coming of the Messiah. Or maybe it was because she didn't know what to do with her broken heart except give it to God.

Anna had only been married a few years when her husband died. She would have experienced sorrow, grief, anguish, and possibly anger. Those are powerful emotions involving an incredible amount of energy. What was she going to do with those emotions? What if she did nothing? Would she be overwhelmed by them? Would she feel as though her life was over? Would life lose its glow?

While she didn't have a choice about what had happened, she had a choice about her response. She chose to live a life devoted to God by being in the temple day after day. She took her sorrow and gave it to God. She took the emotional energy her sorrow demanded and redirected it through prayer and fasting. As she turned her heart toward God, her worship became greater than her wound.

Worship greater than your wound

This phrase is not original with me. I picked it up when I attended an irritating breakout session at a large gathering. The session leader, a psychologist, took up most of the 45 minutes he had been allotted to describe a woman client of his. She had a very sordid background. He told us way more than I ever wanted to know about anyone! Like most conference attendees, I wanted principles and advice, but the psychiatrist droned on and on about all that had happened to this woman. I impatiently tapped my pencil and wondered, *Why is he doing this?*

At the end of the breakout session, he described the end of his therapy session with the woman, when he asked her, "Is your worship greater than your wound?" And then he dismissed us. *That was it*, I remember thinking. *That's all he has to say to us. And I paid good money to be here?* But in the days following the gathering, the psychiatrist's irritating conclusion became a cognitive itch.

Is your worship greater than your wound? The question kept coming to mind. As I reflected about the woman's background I realized she would have had to change her focus if she was going to pull out of her slough of despondency. No matter how awful the past was, she couldn't have a life of any quality if she continued to reside there. Worshipping God, the psychiatrist was suggesting, was the way to move out of the slough and embrace the future.

I don't know if the woman ever did—the psychiatrist didn't have time to tell us what happened to her!—but I believe that is what Anna may have done. The plight of a widow in Anna's day was about the bleakest a woman could experience, and yet Anna ended up with a full life and meaningful work to do because she chose to let go of her sorrow and worship God.

When worship is greater

Anna could have been very bitter about the devastating loss she experienced at such a young age; it is the kind of thing that could turn a woman away from the Lord. She could have cried out in anguish over life's unfairness: Why me? Why now?

When death ravaged her home, Anna made God's house her dwelling place. Night and day she was at the temple. "When as a young, motherless wife, God withdrew from her the earthly love she rejoiced in, she did not bury her hope in a grave."[2] Rather she placed her hope in God.

When she could have seethed with anger over being left desolate with no one to care for her or to protect her, she prayed and asked God for His help. She trusted God. She devoted herself to Him who had promised to be a husband to the widow (see Isaiah 54:4–5).

When she could have dwelt on her loss, she listened with sympathy to others talk about their losses and disappointment. She understood their concerns and responded by praying and fasting for them.

As the years stacked up, she could have resented them. As aging took away the bloom and the strength of her body, it could have taken away her zest for life and left her feeling useless and unproductive. Anna chose to respond to aging the same way she chose to respond to sorrow by devoting herself to God. Instead of becoming discontented or resentful, she maintained her sense of wonder by daily connecting with God.

When she could have been overwhelmed by loneliness and haunted by memories of happier days, she interacted with those who came to the temple. She did not dwell on her own misery. As a result, God gave her a full and meaningful life and increased her spiritual sensitivity.

Sorrow can produce bitterness and resentment, but sorrow can also produce faith, peace and purpose. Out of her sorrow there came serenity, graciousness, and closeness to God. These same outcomes are possible for any woman if she chooses to give her heartache to God and focus on Him. This is something every woman needs to know.

Good to know

At some time or other, most women will eventually be confronted with loss, sorrow and disappointments. By nature, we are relationship-oriented, and relationships change. Disruptions occur. Friends change or move away. Divorces occur; loved ones die. Sometimes our relationships are so important to us that their loss feels like death itself.

Sometimes the losses are intangible, but nevertheless painful. Dreams fail to materialize. Assumptions about life or about others are shattered.

At any one of these times it would be easy to become bitter, resentful, cynical and hard, but Anna's example shows us another way—a way of serenity, peace and purpose. It means taking the anguish and hurt of our sorrow and redirecting that energy in worshipping God.

Your reaction might be, but I can't spend all my time fasting and praying! I can't be at the church all the time! You don't have to do either in order to follow Anna's example.

To pattern our lives after hers doesn't mean we have to respond in exactly the same way Anna did. Worship is attributing worth to God. This could be engaging in ceremonies that honor and glorify Him. It could be praying and fasting as Anna did. It could also be serving others in His name, which has been the Anna-pattern for me.

When my oldest sister died in 1999, it seemed like I entered a new stage in life—a stage where the drama being played out involved recurring losses and challenges. My troubles weren't any greater than anyone else's. Some of them were tangible losses so if I shared them with you, I would gain your sympathy. Some of them were intangible, things you probably would not empathize with, but they were *my* losses and *my* disappointments. Whether they were minimal or major in anyone else's eyes, they made me sad. The sheen of life was being scraped off and leaving nothing but painful reality.

I would have survived—there was never a question about that—but I wanted more than survival. I wanted to still experience God, I wanted a productive and meaningful life, and I wanted to maintain my sense of wonder (more about that in the last two chapters). None of this would have been possible, unless I followed Anna's example. I'm involved in women's missions and ministries, and that's how I keep my focus on Him. And in return, He blesses me just as He did Anna.

Anna's reward

As people came and went, listening to her wisdom, asking for her prayers, she had vital interaction with people. There was much mingling and conversation with men, women, families and travelers in the Court of the Gentiles. From near and far, people came to the temple to worship, offer sacrifices, and observe the religious festivals of Judaism. It was Anna's privilege to pray for them and to minister the Word.

One of the temple visitors I'm sure she liked to converse with was another old person like herself. Simeon had been around the temple for a long time. He was a godly man who was often at the temple although he didn't live there as Anna did. One of the reasons she probably liked to talk with him was because he was waiting "for the Consolation of Israel" (Luke 2:25 NKJV), meaning the fulfillment of Jewish messianic hopes. "The Holy Spirit was with him and had assured him that he would not die before he had seen the Lord's promised Messiah" (Luke 2:25–26 GNT). They talked about when the moment would be and what the Messiah would be like.

One day as she was leaving the Court of Women to go out to greet visitors coming to the temple, she noticed Simeon talking with a couple with a tiny baby. The couple had two pigeons. Anna smiled. This must be a new baby, and the couple was there to observe the ceremony of the redemption of the firstborn and the mother's purification rite. After giving birth, a woman was considered unclean for 40 days if the baby was a boy, and for 80 days if the baby was a girl. At the end of that time she had to bring to the temple a lamb for a burnt offering and a young pigeon for a sin offering to be declared clean.[3] If she could not afford the lamb, she might bring another pigeon. So two pigeons let Anna know why this couple and their baby were there.

I'm sure that at times like this, Anna always liked to greet and to encourage the parents, so as her custom was, she moved toward them. Parents always seemed to appreciate her comments and blessings, and besides, this would usually give her a chance to hold the baby. Right now Simeon was holding the baby, but she knew she would have her opportunity.

As she came near, she heard Simeon say, "With my own eyes I have seen your salvation, which you have prepared in the presence of all peoples: A light to reveal your will to the Gentiles and bring glory to your people Israel" (Luke 2:30–32 GNT).

Anna's heart quickened; this was He! This was the One! Somehow she hadn't expected the Messiah to come as a baby. Maybe it was because everyone associated the Messiah with riches, power and worldly splendor. We've been looking for a great champion like King David who would descend upon the earth and deliver us from the Romans, but here He is as a baby!

As she took the baby from Simeon and held Him in her arms, Anna knew for a certainty that Jesus was the Messiah. There was no "let me think about it" or "I need to give this some consideration," or "I'll get back to you." Here was *the* Messiah in her arms as a tiny baby, and she *knew* Him. She knew Him because she was spiritually ripe. Simeon had a promise that he had clung to through the years, but Anna hadn't. She had clung to God and so she could recognize God's Son when He appeared

She was spiritually perceptive because her heart had been made ripe and ready. Anna's devotion was not hit-or-miss—she wasn't one day "spiritually on" and then the next day "spiritually off." There are insights and blessings and power that come to the person who is constantly devoted that the "sometimes" spiritual—"it's an emergency, God, please help"—kind of pray-er will never know. Anna never ceased to worship. Through out her long widowhood, Anna was unswerving in devotion to Him, and God rewarded her by giving Himself.

She gave thanks to the Lord for getting to witness this; her heart was full and overflowing. She proclaimed glad tidings to those who were also looking for the Messiah. Her years of faithful worship were ". . . rewarded and she became the first female herald of the Incarnation to all who looked for the Redeemer in Jerusalem."[4]

Becoming a *wonder* woman

At some point, Anna had to let go of her grief to focus on God. What other kinds of things might a woman need to let go of to fully worship God?

What is fasting? Should fasting be a part of every Christian's life?

How would Anna's life experiences helped her as a prophetess and as a pray-er?

What are some spiritual disciplines Christians can use to facilitate their turning their sorrow over to God?

Who is the oldest woman you know? Would you consider going to her for prayer? Why or why not?

How do you want to serve the Lord when you are an older woman?

Chapter Seven

MARTHA

You Served How Many?

Luke 10:38–42; John 11:1–44; 12:1–8

How would you like to have your life evaluated from only three scenes? What three scenes would you select? Would you select scenes that show you in the best light? What scenes would best characterize you as a person?

After Dan Rather made a journalistic mistake (the one involving false papers regarding President Bush) and before he left *CBS Evening News*, he participated in a radio panel discussion on journalistic issues that also featured Tom Brokaw and Peter Jennings. Jennings told him not to worry about the mistake. "No one," he said, "is ever remembered for just one incident in his life."

As I listened, I said out loud, "Oh, yeah? Martha is." Even though she is in three biblical scenes, one scene overshadows the others and defines who she is for many people. It is the first scene—the one in which she loses her cool.

Scene 1: Guess who is coming to dinner? (Luke 10:38–42)

Jesus, a celebrity, was with His disciples on the way to Jerusalem when Martha invited Him to her home. Crowds followed Him and tension surrounded Him almost everywhere He went by this time in His ministry. Earlier Jesus had sent out seventy disciples into the villages and towns of Judea. Perhaps some of them told Martha about Jesus, adding to the stories she had already heard. Perhaps she was intrigued, so she told the disciples, "The next time Jesus is in Bethany on His way to Jerusalem, plan on His coming to my house."

Martha saw having Jesus in her home as an opportunity to bring some refreshment to His life as He came near Bethany where she lived, and it would give her and her siblings a chance to know Him better. Martha was a single woman, possibly a homeowner (see Luke 10:38). Her brother, Lazarus, and her sister, Mary, lived with her.

But, even with the best of intentions, things don't always turn out the way you plan. Sometimes what you plan turns out to be more work than you had anticipated, which is what may have happened to Martha.

Among Jews, showing hospitality to a traveling teacher was a special privilege. Recognizing the importance of the occasion and Jesus's celebrity status, Martha wanted to do her best. She wanted to please Him so she began fixing lots of food, fluffing the cushions, looking for serving pieces, and finding a place for everyone to sit, as this invitation may have included Jesus's disciples.

No one stepped forth to help Martha. Where was Lazarus? And where was Mary? Just when Martha really needed her sister, there she was sitting at Jesus's feet, listening to Him teach. Why was she not helping?

As we picture this scene, we might find it easy to assume that Mary and Jesus were in the living room relaxing while Martha was stewing over a hot stove in the kitchen, but we cannot be sure. Most Judean houses consisted of only one room, which served as living room, dining room, and bedroom. The cooking was done outside on an open fire. Martha would have had the frustration of trying to concentrate with people around her, with teaching going on (teaching that she would have liked to have been a part of) and running in and out to tend to the fire. As beads of perspiration popped out on her forehead, thoughts of "all *she* was responsible for" played over and over in her mind. She became "cumbered about much serving" (Luke 10:40 KJV). Finally, she couldn't stand it any longer. Martha—hot, frazzled, and resentful—erupted.

Martha said to Jesus, "Lord, don't you care that my sister has left me to do all the work by myself? Tell her to come and help me!" (Luke 10:40 GNT).

Responding to her outburst, Jesus affectionately replied, "Martha, Martha," and then he validated her feelings: "You are worried and upset over so many things." He had been paying attention; what she was doing had not gone unnoticed. He was not indifferent to Martha's needs, yet in regard to her behavior He could only reprove her. Those "many things" such as the dishes she was preparing had gotten the best of Martha. Jesus said that ultimately, "only one thing is needed. Mary has chosen what is better, and it will not be taken away from her" (Luke 10:42 NIV).

As a result of this incident, Martha's name and personality have become synonymous with busyness. I did an Internet search by typing in simply "Martha busyness"—only those two words—and more than 47,000 entries popped up. This one scene in her life defines her, even though there is more to Martha than busyness, as we'll see in the next two scenes from her life.

Scene 2: Guess who isn't coming? (John 11:1-44)

Leaving Martha's house, Jesus went on to Jerusalem, then into the countryside of Judea. Because of the increasing hostility of the Jews, Jesus and the disciples transferred their ministry to Perea, another province of Palestine. While Jesus was there, Mary and Martha sent him a message about Lazarus: "Lord, the one you love is sick" (John 11:3 NIV).

Jesus sent a message back to them. "The final result of this sickness will not be the death of Lazarus; this has happened in order to bring glory to God, and it will be the means by which the Son of God will receive glory" (John 11:4 GNT).

The next few days must have challenged Martha's faith, because in spite of what Jesus had said, Lazarus died. Was Jesus wrong? It must have seemed that way to her. What else could she think? If Jesus had been wrong about this, how could she be sure He was right about other things? How could she trust His teaching?

We could hardly blame Martha if she had felt this way, but when Jesus arrived in Bethany a few days later, He found her confidence in Him intact. Hearing that Jesus was coming, Martha, ever the leader and protector, rushed out to greet Him, giving Mary time to grieve with her friends in the house.

Never hesitant to speak her mind, Martha expressed her confidence in Jesus even though it was tinged with accusation. She said, "Lord, if you had been here, my brother would not have died" (John 11:21 NIV). Martha knew that Jesus had already raised at least one person from near death, the son of a Capernaum government official (John 4:46–54). She knew He had the power to give life and she recognized that God was still at work in Jesus. She said, "But I know that even now God will give you whatever you ask" (John 11:22 NIV).

"Jesus said to her, 'Your brother will rise again.' Martha answered, 'I know that he will rise again in the resurrection at the last day'" (John 11:23–24 NIV).

In response to her expressions of faith, Jesus made an astounding claim. "He said to her, 'I am the resurrection and the life. He who believes in me will live, even though he dies; and whoever lives and believes in me shall never die'" (John 11:25-26a NIV).

Jesus's claim was shocking—almost unbelievable. Yet when He said to Martha, "Do you believe this?" (John 11:26 NIV), she responded with the most dramatic confession recorded up to this point in the Book of John. She said, "Lord, I believe that you are the Christ, the Son of God, who was to come into the world" (John 11:27 NIV).

The significance of her statement becomes apparent when we remember Peter's confession of faith at Caesarea Philippi. When Jesus asked His disciples, "Who do you say I am?" Peter answered, "Thou art the Christ the Son of the Living God" (Matthew 16:16 KJV).

In the Book of Mark, Peter's statement is the primary confession of faith and the pivotal point in the narrative. In

John's Gospel (whose narrative does not contain Peter's confession) it is made by Martha. "As Peter's confession stands as the pivotal midpoint in Mark, so Martha's confession stands at the climactic midpoint in John. Thus, in John's Gospel, the proclamation of Jesus's identity is made by Martha. Hers is an incredible confession that affirms an incredible claim."[1]

As remarkable as her faith was, though, Martha didn't stop being Martha. She remained a woman concerned about people and the details of life. After her conversation with Jesus, she thought of Mary. She returned to the house and told her, "The Teacher is here and is asking for you."

When Jesus, along with Martha and Mary and others, went to Lazarus's tomb, He commanded the men to roll back the stone over the mouth of the cave. Martha was aware of one of those details others were overlooking. She protested, "There will be a bad smell, Lord. He has been buried four days!" (John 11:39 GNT).

Scene 3: Guess who is overlooked at dinner? (John 12:1–8)

After raising Lazarus, Jesus left Bethany, spent some time in the wilderness of Judea, went back to Galilee for a brief visit, and then returned to Perea. Six days before Passover, Jesus returned to Bethany. After three years of ministry, Jesus had friends and He had enemies. Some of His friends welcomed Him back to the Jerusalem-Bethany area at this time of festivity. They held a banquet in His honor. Martha, Mary, and Lazarus, among others, were there. The host was Simon, a leper whom Jesus had healed.

As the male guests sat around the table, they laughed and talked while they listened to Jesus. The women who were present listened as they hung out around the edges of the banquet room, worked with the food and served the guests. Jesus brought them up to date on where He had been and what He had done since Lazarus' resurrection, and the listeners hung on to His every word. As they reveled in his presence and laughed at his lighter comments, they also sensed an undercurrent of uneasiness in the room. Unspoken questions seemed to float on the air: What next? What is going to happen next?

The people present were aware that Jesus's raising of Lazarus from the dead had upset the religious leaders in Jerusalem. Jesus's miraculous act was evidence against a tenet that many of them held: there was no such thing as the resurrection of the dead. They were not only after Jesus, they wanted to kill Lazarus, too, "because on his account many Jews were rejecting them and believing in Jesus" (John 12:11 GNT).

The people there for dinner also continued to hear echoes of the continual heckling and ridicule that Jesus experienced. So while they were glad to see Jesus, they also felt like they were sitting on the edge of danger, as if something awful might happen next.

Mary picked up on the mood; she sensed the danger and understood. She knew Jesus would soon die. Wanting to do something for him, something that would allow her to show Jesus that she understood, she washed His feet with her perfume and wiped them with her hair, as if she were anointing His body for burial.

And where was Martha? It is easy to overlook her, as you get caught up in the tension of the moment and Mary's beautiful anointing of Jesus for burial. Mary was clearly the star. All eyes were focused on her. Just a little phrase describes Martha and her role. The Bible said, "Martha served" (John 12:2 NIV). Martha served while Mary anointed Jesus and Lazarus reclined at the table with the other banquet guests. That time she said nothing and she let Mary fully enter into the moment without interfering.

From these three scenes, how would you evaluate Martha? I have learned enough about her that I want her on my *wonder* women list.

Super Servant

Within the three biblical scenes in Martha's life, there is one where Martha lost her cool, one where she exhibited strong faith, and one where she quietly served at a banquet. Which one is she most remembered for? It is for her outburst, when she became "cumbered about with much serving" while Jesus was a guest at her house. Because of her "uncool" moment, you may be surprised that Martha is on my *wonder* women list, but she is. She's there because I have to say about her, "Isn't she a *wonder*?"

Isn't she a wonder? Imagine inviting Christ home for dinner! It was Jesus, the Nazarene, the one whom many were saying was *the* Messiah. It was nervy of her. Some believers may not have wanted to risk raising the ire of the Pharisees. Others may have felt like they didn't have lodging fit for a celebrity or couldn't furnish the food. Martha is to be commended for wanting to entertain Jesus, wanting to know Him better, and wanting to open her home to Him.

Isn't she a wonder to be concerned about her brother and sister? She was a loving sister to Lazarus and Mary, sharing her home with them. She provided a structure for

Mary to get to be who she was. Mary got to sit at Jesus's feet because Martha invited Him to her house. Mary had the chance to wash Jesus's feet because Martha was serving the banquet.

Isn't she a wonder to be willing to serve so many guests? At her home, the disciples probably came with Jesus. When Lazarus died, the house was full of mourners. When Simon gave a banquet for Jesus, she said, "Let me help." Martha truly had a servant's heart.

Isn't she a wonder that she continued to serve even after she was rebuffed by Jesus? Jesus's rebuke of Martha is not to imply that practical service is unimportant. Martha's service was important. On other occasions, Jesus had much to say about practical service and the Bible has much to say about servanthood and hospitality. Rather, Jesus's rebuke was a call for understanding and balance. Still, the words had a sting to them, and I admire Martha for learning from the experience and not letting it affect her relationship with Jesus.

Isn't she a wonder that her angry outburst didn't keep her from developing as a believer or keep her from serving again? She could have been ashamed of her emotional eruption and sworn she wasn't going to get involved again. Let someone else do the entertaining, she could have told herself. She could have been embarrassed by her behavior and concluded she never wanted to take any risks again. She could have been hurt by Jesus's remark and withdrawn emotionally from Him, but she didn't. She continued to serve.

Martha's story shows us that she was a responsible woman, a leader, capable of looking after the needs of others and of growing in the process. She was a woman who blundered and made a mistake and yet still was a woman of developing faith, and this is what means the most to me about her life.

Grace to grow

When my book *Can Martha Have a Mary Christmas?* came out, I was anxious to see people's responses. As soon as I could, I made it a part of my book table display at a woman's conference, and I stood by to watch. A woman came up, picked up the book, and looked at the front cover where Martha is entangled in Christmas tree lights. She laid the book down and said, "Humph, nice title, but I'm not a Martha."

I said, "I'll bet you have all your Christmas shopping done" (this was October) and she said, "Yes, I do, and all the presents are wrapped."

This well-organized woman didn't want to be associated with someone who could lose her cool like Martha. She was a woman who had her life under control; she was organized; she was not a Martha.

Well, *I* am like Martha. I lose my cool at times. I've gotten angry at my husband and my sons when they didn't notice how hard I was working to get a holiday meal on the table. I've gotten upset with women who didn't help me with mission projects or do their part in planning an event. I've walked out on a Vacation Bible school class of teenagers who became unruly. I've abruptly left a committee meeting when I was reprimanded by the pastor. Need I give any more examples?

And yet as wrong as I might have been—and I must say these reactions were not planned, nor do I think Martha's was—they did not keep me from experiencing God's grace and growing as a believer in Jesus Christ. Within me both Marthas reside—the Martha of the "make her help me" mentality and the Martha who said to Jesus, "I believe you are the Messiah the Son of God." Through God's grace and forgiveness, I can continue to grow as a believer even when I get cumbered about with much serving. My faith can improve and grow stronger.

I'd like to think because I've learned from my blunders and learned from Martha that I won't lose my cool again, but I can't guarantee it. What I can guarantee is that I won't let it get me down; I won't stop developing as a woman of faith, because Martha is my hero. Losing her cool didn't stop her and it won't stop me from declaring my faith in Jesus as the resurrection and the life.

Becoming a *wonder* woman

If you were asked to choose three scenes from your life that would represent you as a person, what would those three scenes be?

Which is better worship? Sitting at the feet of Jesus or serving Jesus?

What did Jesus's response to Martha mean? That serving was not important?

How do you explain the fact that we can be women who make mistakes but also be women of faith?

Even with the best of intentions, why is it easy for women who look after details of life to go into overdrive and miss what is most important?

What does Jesus's statement "I am the resurrection and the life" mean to you?

Chapter Eight

PRISCILLA

You Taught Who and Went Where?

Acts 18:1–4, 18–21, 24–28; Romans 16:3–5; 1 Corinthians 16:19; 2 Timothy 4:19

If Martha was a woman who could lose her cool, then Priscilla was the "queen of cool." She gets my vote for the "Woman Who Has It All Together" award. This is true whether you are judging her by first-century standards or twenty-first-century standards. She was a woman of many roles, and she handled them well. Let's throw out our lasso to learn why Priscilla is a *wonder* woman.

Who was Priscilla?

Priscilla lived about twenty years after Martha, after Jesus had died, the Holy Spirit had come, and the gospel was being spread throughout the Roman Empire. The gospel had made it to Rome, the capital of the Empire, and was causing a ruckus among the Jews living there. The emperor Claudius said, "Enough!" and expelled the Jews from the city.

Priscilla and her husband Aquila, who was Jewish, were among those forced to leave Rome. They moved to Corinth and set up shop. They were tent makers and business partners. That piece of information alone earned Priscilla some votes for the "Woman Who Has It All Together" award. Many married couples work together in business or other organizations, but I would find that difficult. For years, I've been telling my husband that when he retires, he will have to rent an office to go to every day. Actually I think the idea sets well with him, too, because we both have our way of doing things, including the dishes! We don't want anyone else interfering with our methods.

Priscilla and Aquila were not that way. They were a cooperative team. Their lives were so intertwined that when they are mentioned in the Bible their names are always together. It is never "Priscilla did this" and "Aquila did that"; it is always "Priscilla and Aquila" or "Aquila and Priscilla." Sometimes Priscilla is referred to as "Prisca," but still her name is paired with Aquila's.

As they were getting their business going in Corinth, they met the apostle Paul who had come to Corinth from a different direction. He was on his second missionary journey. He had just been in Thessalonica, Berea and Athens, and the trip wasn't going well. He was spiritually and emotionally bruised from being run out of Thessalonica and Berea and being challenged by intellectuals in Athens. He expected Timothy and Silas, two of his coworkers whom he left behind in Berea, to eventually join him, but at this time, he was alone. He needed friends and he needed a job. He found both when he met Priscilla and Aquila, who were believers in Jesus Christ.

Occasionally Paul received offerings for support, but most of the time he supported himself by working. In Corinth, alone and without any financial support, Paul went to the area of town where tentmakers were located. Among the stalls, Paul, a tentmaker, met Priscilla and Aquila and found what he was looking for—comfort, understanding, and employment! Priscilla and Aquila hadn't been looking, but they found new roles and adventures as their lives intertwined with Paul's, starting in their own home.

Open home, open heart

"From the very beginning Prisca and Aquila were people who kept an open heart and an open door."[1] They opened their home to Paul and his acquaintances and to churches in places where they lived.

Not only did Priscilla and Aquila give Paul a job, they took him in as a houseguest, an ever-present one. No matter how much you want to have a houseguest or houseguests; their added presence adds stress to the household—especially to the hostess, as our discussion of Martha has illustrated. There's more food to buy and cook. There are more dishes to wash and laundry to do, and you lose some of your personal space and feel like you have to wear a "company" personality.

Unless Priscilla had household servants, the stress would have been greater for her than Aquila. Both women and men are hospitable, but women more often feel a greater sense of responsibility with regard to hospitality. This would have been especially true back then when there was a more distinct division between "women's work" and "men's work" than there is today. Even if Aquila shared the physical work of attending to a guest, he probably would not have shared Priscilla's concerns. Would Paul feel at home? What did he like to eat? Did she feed him enough? How could she keep the house neat?

As an experienced traveler, Paul stayed in enough homes that he was probably efficient about looking after himself, so in that sense he probably made a good guest. But Paul also attracted his own guests. Paul's mission was to win men and women to Christ so he engaged people in dialogue wherever he was, on the job, in the marketplace, or after synagogue services. Many of those conversations couldn't be finished at the moment, so it was natural for Paul to say, "I'm staying with Aquila and Priscilla. Why don't you stop by later? We can talk more about it then."

"Well, won't that be an imposition on Priscilla?"

"No, she won't mind. What's another mouth to feed?"

Some of those people Paul invited to "drop in" were probably not—how shall we say it?—the most desirable of house guests. Corinth was an "anything goes" type of town, a wicked city noted for its drunkenness and debauchery. Some of the people who came by—and who later became believers—were fornicators, idolaters, adulterers, thieves, drunkards, revilers and swindlers (see 1 Corinthians 6:9–11).

Priscilla invited them in and made them feel at home. Around her table she accommodated Paul's discussion groups and cleaned up after the guests were gone. Priscilla was a sensitive Christ follower, and she knew that having unhurried dialogue in the warm, receptive environment of a home was conducive to birthing new Christians. As the number of converts grew, they began meeting together on a regular basis. They became a church and needed a place to meet, and the door to Priscilla's home opened wider to accommodate them. She didn't know it at the time, but this was going to become the pattern for her and Aquila's life.

They were in Corinth when they first opened the doors of their home to be the meeting place for the church. The whole idea of having a church was such a new thing that homes were the natural place to meet; it would be years down the road before there would be church buildings. But at that time, baptized believers met together in people's homes, breaking bread together, studying, fellowshipping, and worshipping as a body. Perhaps due to their association with Paul this was a natural development for Priscilla and Aquila. Or perhaps their home was a little larger than some. Because they were business owners, they might have been able to afford a house larger than most. Either way, the church met at their house in Corinth.

When Paul left Corinth after eighteen months, he took Priscilla and Aquila with him to Ephesus, where once again they used their home as a meeting place for the church. Once more Priscilla graciously opened her home to accommodate curious visitors, new converts, and growing Christians. This meant receiving people from many different backgrounds. She didn't put a sign on her door that said, "Only people who have totally cleaned up their act can enter." Ephesus attracted visitors from far and wide, including criminals, so Priscilla welcomed them as visitors, just as she did pious believers from the synagogue.

When the emperor, Claudius—the one who had forced them out of Rome—died, Priscilla and Aquila returned to their hometown. They established a church there. When Paul wrote his long letter to the Romans, he said, "Greet Priscilla and Aquila, my fellow workers in Christ Jesus. . . . Greet also the church that meets at their house" (Romans 16:3, 5 NIV).

Then once again, Priscilla and Aquila were forced to leave Rome. This time it was due to the tyrannical emperor Nero, who gleefully persecuted Christians. As Nero had Christians tortured and executed for refusing to denounce their faith, God led Priscilla and Aquila back to Ephesus, where once again they opened their home for ministry.

Wherever Priscilla and Aquila went, their home was a center of Christian fellowship, learning, and service. They radiated friendship, acceptance and love. "Sometimes we think of a home as a place with a shut door, a place in which we can go and shut the door and keep the world out: but equally a home should be a place with an open door. The open door, the open hand, and the open heart"[2] were certainly characteristics of Priscilla and Aquila's life. This doesn't mean it was easy for them, but the nature of the blessings they experienced far exceeded the stress.

Blessed not stressed

Once when I was interviewing a group of women for a possible book on the stages of life, a woman in her early sixties said, "I thrive on seeing babies born."

I had hardly expected an answer like that and assumed she worked in a hospital or was a midwife. She went on to explain that her joy was bringing people into the kingdom of God, seeing sinners born again. I can understand that kind of joy, and when you experience it, all the stress that one might have experienced in the birthing fades. I imagine it was that way for Priscilla. Sure, having Paul as a houseguest and opening her home to others meant work, but it also meant joy that rubs out the stress. With people coming and going and with the church meeting in her home, any time Priscilla might see a new convert being born! Now that was something to live for!

It was also mentally and spiritually stimulating to have Paul around and to have people of different backgrounds coming and going. Priscilla learned from Paul as he talked with others in her home and in the synagogue where he held discussions. In the synagogue, the men and women were seated separately and the women weren't allowed to say anything, but Priscilla listened closely. She absorbed what Paul said, but still she had questions, and at her home, she could ask them.

As they broke bread together, Priscilla had the opportunity to ask Paul questions: "Where have your travels taken you, Paul? When did you first meet Christ? What was it like to come face to face with the resurrected Jesus? What have you learned since in following Christ? What have your troubles and trials taught you about the nature of the Christian life? How does the Holy Spirit work in our lives?"

As their lives became intertwined, Paul recognized the spiritual growth in Priscilla and Aquila, so he asked them to go with him when he left Corinth. Paul planned to be in Jerusalem for Passover and then go to Antioch of Syria to report to the church that had commissioned him as a missionary. On board ship they continued their discussions.

Sometimes it was just the three of them. Other times it included other travelers on board. Paul continued as *the teacher*, but the time was coming when Priscilla and Aquila would be teachers too.

Priscilla, the teacher

Their ship docked in Ephesus, a city with a large Jewish population. As was his custom, Paul headed for the synagogue where he reasoned with the Jews. He said enough to whet their appetite. They said, "Please stay with us longer. We want to hear more."

Paul responded, "God willing, I will try to come back sometime. In the meantime, I'll tell you what I will do; I'll leave two knowledgeable people here with you. They can tell you about Christ. These are my coworkers, Priscilla and Aquila."

It is hard to tell from the Bible whether Paul had planned all along to leave Priscilla and Aquila in Ephesus or whether he suddenly realized how knowledgeable and capable they were. In his haste, though, Paul forgot that his authority as a teacher was different from Priscilla and Aquila's. Paul was a rabbi, so he was free to expound in the synagogue, but Priscilla and Aquila were lay people and Priscilla was a woman. They could not be teachers in the synagogue, but they could teach in their own home and so you won't be surprised to find that they opened their home to learners, including a scholar from Egypt.

Showing a more accurate way

Apollos, a brilliant speaker and Jewish scholar from Alexandria, Egypt, was an eloquent man who knew how to use language correctly and convincingly. He also was very knowledgeable about the Hebrew Scriptures, what we think of as the Old Testament. He knew how to use and apply biblical principles as well as teach them to others, which he did with great zeal and fervor. Such a man might not seem to need a teacher himself, but Apollos did.

When he spoke boldly in the synagogue in Ephesus, Priscilla and Aquila heard him. As they listened to him, they realized he didn't have a complete understanding of the Christian message. Apollos "had been instructed in the Way of the Lord, and with great enthusiasm he proclaimed and taught correctly the facts about Jesus. However, he knew only the baptism of John" (Acts 18:25 GNT).

In other words, in Egypt, he had not heard the full gospel story. He knew about John the Baptist preparing the way for Jesus and the baptism of repentance that he preached. He believed that Jesus was the Messiah but he didn't know about Christ's death and resurrection, and certainly not about the coming of the Holy Spirit at Pentecost.

"When Priscilla and Aquila heard him, they invited him to their home and explained to him the way of God more adequately" (Acts 18:26 NIV). They taught Apollos about Jesus's death, resurrection, and His Holy Spirit. As a result, Apollos was strengthened as a believer and as a teacher. From Ephesus he went on to Achaia (where Corinth is located). He was a great help to the Christian community because "with his strong arguments he defeated the Jews in public debates by proving from the Scriptures that Jesus is the Messiah" (Acts 18:28 GNT).

Apollos could have been intimidating to any lay teacher. He was bold, fervent, passionate, and knowledgeable. In a day when women weren't given much freedom to speak and to teach, Priscilla could have ignored Apollos's incomplete knowledge. But she had learned from Paul the importance of keeping the gospel pure and true. Paul was always going up against false teachers who wanted to compromise the gospel. Later, Paul would warn the Ephesian elders about just such a possibility occurring among them.

Some scholars assume that Priscilla initiated Apollos's instruction since her name is mentioned first. If that is true, she did it very tactfully. After all, she could have encouraged Aquila to question Apollos. "Honey, you go up there and confront Apollos since I am not allowed to speak in the synagogue. That man is not telling the complete story. Make sure he gets it right." Her reasoning could have been that if he wasn't teaching correctly, he needed to be exposed! She could have encouraged Aquila to interrupt Apollos, interrogate him publicly—get the issues out in the open. That approach certainly would have done that, but a potentially great teacher might have been embarrassed, humiliated and lost to the kingdom of God. It might have discouraged him from speaking and it might have kept Apollos from learning "the rest of the story" about Jesus, and what a loss that would have been!

Priscilla was a woman who saw the bigger picture. She grasped what God was trying to do and got on board; there were others riding the same train and she joined them and cooperated with them rather than insisting on her rights. Her thinking wasn't, What can God do for *me*? Rather her concern was, What can I do for God? We see this helpful spirit in how she worked with her husband, with Paul and with the church. She was a solid marriage partner, a team player and a good friend.

Cooperative spirit

Priscilla and Aquila give us an example of how well two people can work together when both are committed. In early New Testament times women were considered intellectual inferiors, and in "religious matters, most wives were addenda to their husband's faith."[3] Priscilla never seemed to be merely an addendum to Aquila. Theirs was a true partnership. Their names were always linked together. Sometimes his name was first; others times her name was first. They had a business together, they worked together, they opened their home together, and together they learned from Paul.

Priscilla and Aquila were not merely companions of Paul, watching him as he preached. They joined in the labor of ministry with him. Paul referred to them as "my fellow workers in Christ Jesus" (Romans 16:3 NIV). They worked with Paul and greatly aided his ministry. They opened their home to Paul, facilitated his teaching, supported his ministry, followed his direction, and stood by him when others deserted him. Priscilla and Aquila even risked their lives for Paul (see Romans 16:4*a*), even though the Bible doesn't tell us specifically what happened. I wish it had! That must have been quite a story.

One of the last messages that Paul wrote was a greeting to this pair of Christians who had come through so much with him (see 2 Timothy 4:19). Other coworkers had deserted him, but they were true and faithful friends to the end.

Priscilla has become a friend of mine, too. Surprising, isn't it? A woman who sometimes loses her cool has became friends with the queen of cool. Priscilla was a woman of many roles and she handled them well. Priscilla is who I want to be when I grow up. She remains a model for me as I juggle my own roles.

In my study of Priscilla, I couldn't find one negative comment. There's not even a hint of a blemish on her record, so it would be easy to write her off as someone impossible to be like, certainly not anyone to feel close to. That might have been the case even if I hadn't seen into her heart. Any woman who has room for the criminal element of Ephesus, for the drunkards of Corinth, for the scholar from Egypt, and for Paul the mighty missionary has room for me. She's a woman with an open door and an open heart, and she says to me, "Come on in, Brenda. Make yourself at home, and let's talk about what it means to be a Christian."

Becoming a *wonder* woman

How many roles did Priscilla have? What were some of them?

What are your roles? What did you find difficult about handling so many roles?

How can couples or families serve God together?

What are the difficulties in serving God together?

What's good about serving God together?

What would you find difficult about opening your home to others? What would make it worthwhile for you to do so?

Chapter Nine

PHOEBE

You Traveled All That Way Alone?

Romans 16:1–2

If you could go anywhere in the world, where would you want to go? I'm always uncomfortable in social gatherings when this question is posed. I'm a homebody; there's just no place I'd rather be than at home. I guess that's why I have such admiration for Phoebe who traveled alone from Cenchrea to Rome. The distance was 800 miles, not a great distance by today's standards, but times—and travel conditions—were much different then. Travel was never done with ease and always with apprehension.

In Phoebe's day

Like Priscilla, Phoebe was one of Paul's coworkers. Phoebe lived in Cenchrea near Corinth where Priscilla first met Paul. While we don't know if the two women ever interacted there, we do know they met when Phoebe arrived in Rome. Paul mentioned both women in his closing words to his letter to the Romans (16:1–4). He was commending Phoebe, his letter carrier, to them and sending greetings to Priscilla and Aquila.

Cenchrea was less than 10 miles west of Corinth (think modern day Greece). Rome was the capital of the vast Roman Empire. To get to Rome, Phoebe would have had to travel by land and by sea.

The most common means of land travel was walking, simply because alternate ways were too expensive for most people. I know we all have these mental images of biblical characters riding horses, camels or even donkeys, but those were usually for the elite. A large selection of wheeled vehicles such as chariots and carriages was available to travelers, but to rent or buy a wheeled vehicle would have been beyond the means of most people. The cost of a horse limited their use "mainly to persons of wealth, government officials, and military personnel."[1] Even though legend has it that the wise men rode camels, they were generally not used because they were expensive, less docile than donkeys, and altogether unreliable. Camels were more often associated with caravans traveling across deserts. People used donkeys to bear their baggage rather than for riding. Donkeys were costly, too, and could be requisitioned by any Roman soldier or official who needed one so the main mode of land travel was by foot.

Walkers were exposed to the elements, to wild animals, and to highway robbers. Generally conditions in the Roman Empire were more secure than they had been for a long, long time thanks to the lingering influence of Caesar Augustus, who stabilized the area, but many local areas had no real power or authority in ridding themselves of criminals. Walkers had very little protection from robbers in rural areas so they tried never to walk alone.

Walkers could count on covering 16 to 25 miles a day depending on the road conditions, the elevation, the weather, and their physical strength. So if you were going a distance greater than that, you would need places to stay at night.

Room in the inn

On the road, travelers usually spent the night in inns. "The average inn was no more than a courtyard surrounded by rooms. Baggage was piled in the open space where animals were also tethered for the night."[2]

Drivers of the wheeled vehicles slept on the ground in the courtyard. It is possible that Phoebe was rich enough—something we'll discuss later in this chapter—to rent a vehicle for the land travel. If she did, her driver took his place along with the others in the courtyard. To keep warm, the drivers built little fires fueled by dried dung. The offensive smell permeated the air and filtered into the rooms of the inn and mixed with the body odors of the roommates.

Yes, that's plural! Travelers didn't rent a room; they rented a bed in a room. This means they didn't know who their roommates were going to be, what they were going to be like—or smell like!—or if they were trustworthy. Many of the inns were not well-kept, but their beds were always occupied by additional roommates—bedbugs!

With the inn conditions they way they were, travelers often depended on people in private residences for lodging, and sometimes they had to if they found themselves at nightfall nowhere near an inn. When they could—when someone could vouch for them—they carried with them letters of recommendation so people would let them stay in their homes. The commendation would introduce the person and testify to his or her character.

Consequently, those people living near the well-traveled Roman roads and in important cities became "over used" in giving hospitality. They grew reluctant to entertain strangers. That may be one reason Paul asked the Christians at Rome to receive Phoebe well and to assist her in any way they could. Without his commendation, she might have been just another person seeking lodging.

Whether Phoebe walked or rode in a wheeled vehicle, she also had to travel by sea, and that had its own set of challenges.

Travel by sea

To get to Rome, Phoebe would have had to sail across the Adriatic Sea to reach Italy. There were no passenger vessels sailing regular schedules so Phoebe would have had to seek a ride on a cargo ship or a grain ship. These ships took passengers on a space available basis and at a good price. Ship owners haggled to get the maximum amount they could for the passenger's fare.

You not only had to have the money to pay the expensive fare, you had to be a patient person to travel by ship. You had to wait for the right weather conditions. At certain times of the year, ships didn't travel at all because of contrary winds. You waited for favorable winds, and when the ship was ready to sail, you had better be near by. No one was going to come looking for you.

No kind of food or services were provided for the passengers except water. You had to bring your food for the entire trip with you, and you had to cook it on board. Passengers "had to cook for themselves, which meant taking turns, after the crew had been fed, at the hearth in the galley. The fire might be doused by a stray wave, or rough conditions might mean the fire had to be extinguished before passengers had finished cooking, since loose live coals could do irreparable damage to a wooden boat in a very short time."[3]

Of course, you may not have wanted to eat, as the rolling and pitching of the ship caused sea sickness. Or you may have had to beat off rats to keep them from attacking your food.

Passengers had to bring their own bedding to live on deck; "there were no cabins on the average coastal vessel. Apart from a little shade thrown by the mainsail, no shelter was provided. The more experienced travelers brought small tents to protect themselves and their provisions."[4]

With the food, the bedding, and possibly a tent, it would have been difficult for Phoebe to carry all this on board the ship and to guard it for the duration of the trip. If she traveled alone, Phoebe was very brave and strong. If she were rich, she may have brought her household servants along, although nothing is said in the Bible about her having assistants.

Phoebe had to be physically strong and hardy to travel by ship, and she also had to be fearless. Travelers went by ship only when there was no real alternative because storms and shipwrecks were common. Paul encountered many of these dangers in his travels. He had been in three shipwrecks and once spent twenty-four hours in the water (2 Corinthians 11:25). One storm at sea he endured was so bad that those on board gave up all hope of being saved (Acts 27:20–21). The Jewish historian, Josephus, told about a ship that went to sea in winter on an urgent military mission and hit three continuous months of storms. Going by ship was so fraught with dangerous possibilities, only urgent needs motivated you to travel by ship.

Phoebe knew the dangers of sea travel since Cenchrea was a port city, and yet she went to Rome. What would have possessed her? Why might she have risked her life and encountered frustrations, discomfort and numerous dangers to make the trip? There are at least four possible reasons.

A business trip

Phoebe might have gone to Rome to take care of business. *Her* business. When Paul encouraged the believers at Rome to receive her, he asked them to "assist her in whatever *business* she has need of you; for indeed she has been a *helper* of many and of myself also" (Romans 16:1–2 NKJV; author's italics).

The implication is that she was a businesswoman who went to Rome for some reason associated with her business. Perhaps there was some legal problem she needed to attend to or a special purchase she needed to make.

Paul's comment about Phoebe being a "helper" also strengthens this implication. From her business, she was wealthy enough to assist others. The Greek word that has been translated "helper" is *prostates*, the feminine form of a noun that can denote a position as leader, president, guardian, champion, protectress, benefactor, or patron. Being a protectress, benefactor, or patron, she may have had ample finances to share.

What kind of business she could have been in? Weren't opportunities for women limited?

She could have been a widow who inherited her husband's business. The fact that her name is not linked to a man's could mean she was a widow without brothers, fathers, or sons. Or it could mean that she was a very important widow, a renowned person in her own right.

But she may not have been a widow. Phoebe was not a Jew, and Greek and Roman women had more freedom than Jewish women to pursue opportunities and to act independently. For example, they were able to own and manage property and, thus, to accumulate wealth; this seems to have been particularly true in the area where Phoebe lived. When Paul was preaching in the synagogue at Thessalonica, some of the Jews were convinced and became believers in Jesus Christ. The Bible says, "and so did many of the *leading women* and a large group of Greeks who worshiped God" (Acts 17:2–4 GNT; author's italics). When he moved on to Berea and preached there, "Many of them believed; and *many Greek women* of high social standing and many Greek men also believed" (Acts 17:12 GNT; author's italics). At his next stop in Athens, a woman who was a part of the Aeropagus court converted to Christianity. So perhaps Phoebe, a Gentile, was a woman like one of these. Perhaps she was an independent single woman of high social standing, who may have owned a business that required her to go to Rome.

Church concerns

Another possibility is that Phoebe needed to go to Rome on church business. Some scholars think the travel and Paul's recommendation are associated with her role as a church worker. That's because Paul described her as "a servant of the church in Cenchrea" (Romans 16:1b NKJV).

The word for "servant" in the Greek is *diakonos*, which could simply mean being a servant in the sense that many believers are and in the sense that Martha served. They give untiringly or unselfishly to the work of the Kingdom, usually in informal and caring ways. But *diakonos* could also be an official title, suggesting a leadership role; hence, some translations call Phoebe a deacon (as the NRSV does) or deaconess (as the *Williams Translation* does and the *NIV* adds in a footnote), doing work similar to what the first deacons did (Acts 6:1–7). If she were a church official, then she might have gone to Rome to confer with the greater Christian community. Perhaps she had counsel that would help them or they might have helpful information for her.

A missionary's call

There's also the possibility that Phoebe was compelled by the urgency of what Christ had done in her life to share her story. *Perhaps* she went to Rome as a missionary.

Paul asked the Roman believers to welcome her "in the Lord in a manner worthy of the saints" (Romans 16:2 NKJV). As we've already noted, being a saint means called out or chosen by God. Perhaps her going to Rome was because God had called her.

Phoebe's home town of Cenchrea was a thriving metropolis with temples of Venus, Aesculapius, and Isis. The church at Cenchrea had probably been an outgrowth of Paul's work in nearby Corinth. "Phoebe" is a Gentile name that comes from Greek mythology. It means "pure" or "radiant as the moon." From hearing the gospel, either from Paul or one of his Corinthian converts, Phoebe left her pagan background to become a pure and radiant light for Jesus. Consequently, she had a story to tell, and she wanted to tell it.

We're not saying she was a professional missionary as Paul was. A woman probably didn't do that in New Testament times as we have no mention of it in the Bible, but that doesn't mean Phoebe couldn't have been called to be a one-time missionary to Rome to share her story.

Women as enthusiastic as Phoebe would have been regarded with suspicion as women were often involved in religious cult leadership, something associated with emotion and frenzy. This would have been reason enough for Paul to urge Roman believers to accept her.

A favor for a friend

Phoebe's going to Rome could simply have been because Paul asked her to go.

Rome was a good place to center the Christian movement. Paul knew that and wanted to go there but he hadn't yet. This church had started without his leadership. He wanted to make sure the Roman followers understood salvation was by faith in Jesus Christ. This was always a concern of his, as churches were constantly threatened by the teachings of false teachers. He also knew the wisdom of having the church's center hub at the Roman capital. God had given him a vision that he eventually would go to Rome but he couldn't go just yet. He needed to get an offering he had been collecting for the Jerusalem churches to them so he did the next best thing—he wrote a letter (what we now call the Book of Romans).

There was no postal system for the general populace of the Roman Empire. The government had its postal system, but ordinary citizens had to find someone to carry their letters. You looked for someone who was "going that way" or you asked someone to make a special trip if the correspondence was crucial.

Paul could have heard that Phoebe was going to Rome on business and asked her to deliver his treatise or he could have asked her to make a special trip to deliver the letter as a favor to him. She was such a reliable worker at the church at Cenchrea that he knew he could count on her to get his letter to Rome. She had helped him before and he was confident she would help him again, so he asked her to deliver his letter.

While we will never know for sure the reason for Phoebe's trip to Rome, considering these four possibilities is important because we may find ourselves in similar situations.

Lassoing Phoebe

In our businesses, in our careers, or with our jobs, we may find opportunities to do God's business. We are never on vacation from being a Christian, so if we find ourselves in another locale because our work takes us there, we can look for opportunities to serve. We may have computer expertise that can assist a mission struggling to bring itself up to date with technology. We may have marketing skills and can help a community center develop a brochure for fundraising purposes. Your having the job you have, giving you opportunities, may be God's way of saying, "Go, use what you have to further My Kingdom."

In striving to be a good church worker, we may find ourselves spreading out beyond our local congregation to have influence in a wider arena where we can share what we have learned and where we can also learn from others. Having had our lives changed by believing in Jesus Christ, we have a story to tell. We may hear God calling us to share our story and His story in other places. True Christ followers understand that they can hear the command "Go" at any time. This doesn't mean all Christ followers will have to go great distances, but it does mean all must be willing to leave the familiar, the routine, and the secure.

In being part of the body of Christ, we may need to assist other believers from time to time just as Phoebe helped Paul. This doesn't mean we have to say "yes" every time another Christian asks us to do something, but it does mean we should prayerfully consider the request. When another Christian asks for assistance, it may be God's way of saying, "Go, help."

Let's face it. Much of our effort in the Christian life goes toward making our lives comfortable and secure, but if we want a wonder-filled life, we may need to move out of our comfort zone. Through traveling for Him—because He's told me to "Go"—I've learned much about myself, about others and about God. Even when it seems like where He is asking me to go or what He is asking me to do is insignificant, I go. You never know what the far-reaching consequences will be when God is behind the command.

Phoebe didn't know. She died never knowing how important this trip was to the future of Christianity. One scholar said, "Phoebe carried under the folds of her robe the whole future of Christian theology." The Book of Romans, like no other document ever written, has influenced the development of Christianity and spelled out the implications of God's saving grace through Jesus Christ. There was no carbon copy or backup file. It was up to Phoebe to get the message to Rome, and she did.

Becoming a *wonder* woman

What has travel taught you about yourself?

What has travel taught you about God?

What has travel taught you about people?

What kind of "Go" commands can a Christian woman expect to hear from God?

If a letter of commendation were written about you, what do you hope it would say?

Three of out of the four *supercapable* women (Anna, Martha, and Phoebe) were unmarried. What spiritual advantages do single women have?

Part 4

SHE DID WHAT?

You begin to think you know your gender pretty well. Then a woman does something that causes you to exclaim, "She did what?" Or if you are talking with her face-to-face, you can't help but ask, "What were you thinking?" What she did just doesn't make sense; it goes against conventional thinking. Her behavior was incredible. You say to yourself, "I have to wonder about her."

In this part of the book, we're going to look at biblical women who exhibited incredible behavior. Their actions were so nervy and out of the ordinary that they make us gasp in astonishment, "They did what?"

We could write these women off—not lasso them for learning—except we might miss some important discoveries about ourselves and the God we serve. Sometimes we are so molded by conformity to cultural and religious expectations that we see things rigidly. Interesting or creative parts of ourselves may be stifled. Some times the incredible behavior of others can shake up our thinking enough to ask, Who is the real me? Who is the God I serve?

Chapter Ten

JAEL

A Stake? You've Got to Be Kidding!

Judges 4:17–18; 4:21–22; 5:6; 5:24–27

If we were likening the Bible's *wonder* women to superheroes, we would have to call Jael Spider-Woman. Like the spider in the old poem "The Spider and the Fly," she saw her "fly" and cleverly lured him into her tent and lulled him to sleep.

The fly

The fly was Sisera, the powerful general of the Canaanites who were oppressing God's people when Deborah was a judge. With her God-given insight, Deborah saw that they needed to go to war, but her general Barak hesitated. The king of the Canaanites, Jabin, had a powerful army that possessed 900 iron chariots, and the Israelites, God's people, had no iron. Their weapons were made of copper, which was too soft to make a sharp sword, a spear or a chariot, and people were terrified of Sisera.

Barak said to Deborah, "I'll fight the Canaanites if you go with me."

"'All right,' she replied, 'I'll go with you; but I'm warning you now that the honor of conquering Sisera will go to a woman instead of to you!'" (Judges 4:9 TLB).

When you read this story for the first time, you assume Deborah will be that woman. After all, she's the woman going to war, but the reader—and Sisera!—are in for a surprise.

Sisera's assumption

When Sisera learned that Deborah, Barak, and 10,000 recruits were ready to fight, he headed out to meet them with his army and his chariots. Underarmed, Deborah's group headed for Mount Tabor where they could see the approaching Canaanites. Someone else also arrived at the scene. It was Heber, the Kenite.

The Kenites were not Israelites, but Midianites, descendants of Moses' father-in-law. The Kenites had long been allies of Israel, but for some reason Heber broke rank and sided with King Jabin. Maybe he just wanted to be identified with the winning side. With its 900 chariots, Jabin's army was sure to be victorious. Or it could be he was developing business. The Kenites were traveling metalsmiths. Heber might have done business with the Canaanites in the past or hoped to get some at the scene. Perhaps in the heat of battle, the chariots would need some repair work, and he would be available to get right to it. It's even possible Heber was the one who tipped off Sisera that the Israelites were gathering forces and heading toward Mount Tabor.

Jael, Heber's wife, went with him to the Mount Tabor

area where they set up camp. She stayed with their tent while he checked out the battle scene.

When Deborah gave the order, Barak led the 10,000 volunteers down the slopes of Mount Tabor into battle. At that time, God suddenly unleashed a heavy rain (Judges 5:4–5). The heavy rain pelted Sisera, his men and charioteers. So violent was the rain that the heavy iron chariots sank deep in the mud.

This unanticipated development caused the Canaanite troops to panic. They abandoned the chariots and started running. The sight energized the Israelite soldiers and they fought even harder, killing the Canaanite chariot drivers and other soldiers. In the ensuing chaos, Sisera saw defeat was imminent. He abandoned his chariot and fled. He ran for his life through the blinding rain, not realizing where he was going, just desperate to get away. He was scared of the Israelite men who were pursuing him, but he wasn't scared of the woman he saw standing in front of a tent. She's just a woman, he thought. What could she do? I'll probably scare her, all to my advantage. She'll help me out, I'm sure.

As he got closer, he saw the woman was Heber's wife. Even better, he thought, she'll be sympathetic. If Heber was an ally, then his wife surely will be too. He assumed he could find refuge in her tent and lay low for awhile until the danger was past.

As Sisera was looking at Jael, she was looking at him. She had finished setting up the tent—something Kenite wives did—and was looking for Heber's return. Instead, she saw Sisera running towards her. This could only mean one thing—the Canaanites were losing. What should she do? How should she respond?

"Said the Spider to the Fly"

Jael immediately sized up the situation when she saw Sisera running toward her. His being alone meant the Israelites must be winning. This also meant Sisera was in trouble. Others would be after him. What could she do? Or what should she do? Like a spider who has just completed building her web, Jael had a secure tent ready to use. How could she lure him in?

Recognizing his breathlessness and sensing his fear, she "said to him, 'Come, my Lord, come right in. Don't be afraid'" (Judges 4:18 NIV).

"I'm sure you must be weary, dear,
with soaring up so high;
Will you rest upon my little bed?"
said the Spider to the Fly."[1]

Sisera readily accepted her invitation. He was relieved. He felt he was safe now. He could stop running, catch his breath, rest, and figure out what to do next. Jael quickly covered him with a blanket, giving Sisera the impression that she was protecting him. It warmed him as he shivered in his damp clothes.

He was not only damp and cold, he was thirsty. He said to Jael, "Please give me some water" (Judges 4:19 NIV). Instead, she opened a skin of milk and gave him a drink—another ploy of hers. Perhaps she knew what most of us know now: Warm milk—and without refrigeration hers would have been warm—raises the body temperature and triggers a slow down response. Milk also contains tryptophan, the same ingredient that makes you sleepy after eating Thanksgiving turkey. Maybe Jael knew he would be sleeping like a baby soon so she tucked him in.

"There are pretty curtains drawn around,
the sheets are fine and thin;
And if you like to rest awhile,
I'll snugly tuck you in!"[2]

As he felt his body relax, he never doubted that he was safe in Jael's hands. He didn't forget, though, that he was soon to be a hunted man, if he wasn't already. "Stand in the doorway of the tent," he told her. "'If someone comes by and asks you, 'Is anyone here?' say 'No.' Tell any inquiring Israelite troops that your tent is empty" (Judges 4:20 NIV).

Feeling certain that she would do what he asked, the battle-weary, milk-filled general quickly went to sleep. It was the deep sleep of someone who could finally relax after a stressful time. He went to sleep believing he was safe, but he wasn't. He underestimated the power of a tent-dwelling woman.

Ready, aim, strike

While Sisera lay sleeping, Jael picked up a tent peg and her mallet. She quietly approached Sisera, put the peg on his temple, and swiftly and accurately drove the peg through his temple into the ground, killing him instantly.

She did what? Your eyes aren't deceiving you. You read that right. "She drove the peg through his temple into the ground, and he died" (Judges 4:21 NIV). When I told Jael's story at a retreat, a woman in the audience gasped audibly. It was no quiet intake of the breath; everyone in the room heard her, and no wonder. It was a gruesome act. How could a woman do something like that?

Killing someone in this manner is certainly uncharacteristic of women. We usually think of men as the ones prone to violence, and for good reason. In the early eighties, anthropologist Melvin Konner wrote, "In every culture there is at least some homicide, in the context of war or ritual or in the context of daily life, and in every culture men are mainly responsible for it. . . Men are more violent than women."[3]

That may be changing in the United States. According to federal statistics, 12.3 percent of homicides are committed by women.[4] But even acknowledging that women can and do kill, it is hard to wrap our minds around the picture of a woman stealthily sneaking up on a sleeping man and driving a stake through his temple. It just goes against our view of women, and it is hard to believe that Jael had the physical strength to sink that peg with one swift blow all the way through Sisera's head and into the ground. "On the average, females are not as strong as males when it comes to muscular strength. Almost 90 percent of a man's weight is strength compared to about 50 percent of a woman's weight. In all human races, women have less muscular strength than men."[5]

Of course, there are always exceptions to generalities about men and women, and Jael could have been an exception to the physical strength observation. As a nomad, she was experienced at putting up tents and securing them to the ground. As she and Heber had moved from place to place, perhaps she had put up so many that she had developed very strong muscles and an accurate aim. It was a good thing, too. If she had missed, if she had driven the stake in part way or too slowly, Sisera might have awakened, figured out what was happening, become enraged and killed her. He wouldn't have thought twice about eliminating someone, particularly an insignificant tent-dwelling woman.

With the risk so great, why did Jael do it? Her people were not in conflict with the Canaanites. Why didn't she just hide Sisera as he asked her to?

The Spider

Jael was a strong, cunning, courageous and confident woman. Why might have motivated her to put herself in harm's way to kill Sisera?

Did she believe she was doing God's will? Jael helped God's people by eliminating their archenemy, but we can't assume Jael had a sense that God was directing her as He did Deborah. Jael was not an Israelite as Deborah was. If God spoke directly to Jael, we have no scriptural evidence that He did.

Did she believe in righting wrongs? Jael had observed the unfair way the Canaanites treated the Israelites. For twenty long years, the Canaanites had oppressed them. They had been years of slavery, of grinding poverty, and of cruel suffering. It was a grossly unfair situation, and when Jael saw Sisera coming toward her, she may have realized she was in a position to change the situation. If he were permitted to escape, the oppression might get even worse. "This meant that Jael herself would have been involved in the guilt of the slaughter of many innocent lives in Sisera's future career of aggression against the" [Israelites].[6] Perhaps she was not ready to shoulder that kind of guilt or bear that kind of responsibility.

Was she being self-protective? Was she thinking, Is it going to be him or me? A warrior retreating in fear from a battlefield and bloodshed who meets a woman in an isolated area is only going to be thinking of his safety. She was in no position to refuse his advances. Had she tried, he would have forced his way into the tent. He would have killed her without giving it a second thought if it meant he was protecting himself from the Israelites.

Did she see this as an opportunity to be a heroine? Maybe as her muscles had grown stronger year after year and her accuracy at hitting the tent pegs had improved, maybe these attributes had gone unappreciated. When Sisera approached her tent, perhaps this was the opportunity to show her stuff—to save the day for the Israelites, to get the man that no one else had been able to get. While this isn't a very lofty motive, it is a possibility, because she is quick to show off her trophy.

She knew someone would come looking for Sisera and so she stood at the door looking. Sure enough, it wasn't long until Barak showed up. Jael stepped out to meet him. "'Come,' she said, 'I will show you the man you're looking for.' So he went in with her, and there lay Sisera with the tent peg through his temple—dead" (Judges 4:22 NIV).

What must Barak have thought? Was he shocked? Had he been thinking all along that Deborah was the woman who would get credit for victory? Now here before him was the dreaded general lying dead, and killed by a tent-dwelling woman! Deborah had said that God would deliver them but never for a moment had Barak thought it would be in this manner. He may have found her act as incredible as we do, but—and here's what's important—God's people were delivered. Consequently, Barak and Deborah found Jael praiseworthy. They called her "most blessed of women" (Judges 5:24*a* NIV) and "most blessed of tent-dwelling women" (Judges 5:24*c* NIV). Not all Bible commentators, though, have agreed with their praise.

Spider-Woman's flaws

The commentators point out what Jael did wrong. Obviously, the most striking wrong is that she committed murder. She broke one of the Ten Commandments. She assassinated a man in cold blood, a soundly sleeping man who was not alert enough to defend himself. One commentator has said her act was morally reprehensible.

She was deceptive with her "spider" ways of luring Sisera into her tent, giving him milk, feigning friendliness, and giving him the impression that he could trust her. She led him to believe that she was going to protect him. By doing so, she violated the basic rule of hospitality. Amazingly, considering how out of control everything was at the time of the judges, hospitality carried with it an almost sacred duty. Once a guest was invited into a home/tent, he was to be protected and cared for even at the expense of everyone else involved.

Obviously, we shouldn't emulate Jael in the same way we do some heroes. In other words, we're not going to read into her story an OK to murder our enemies, no matter how much we might want to! Her story doesn't give us a biblical basis to kill or to be deceptive, just as Rahab's story doesn't teach that we should become prostitutes or lie. I believe, though, we can take heart from Jael's courage. It reminds me that there is always more to women and to God than we might assume or think.

There's always more

Sisera trusted Jael's hospitality. He assumed that she was just going to naturally comply with his wishes because he was *the* powerful general. He also assumed that Jael was with him in spirit as her husband was, but husbands and wives don't always agree on their political favorites.

Like Sisera, we can assume we know women. We can predict what they will do and what they are feeling. And sometimes we are just so certain we have them figured out. But Jael's story reminds us that women may do the unpredictable or may think differently than we do. Each woman, thank God, is unique!

We also make assumptions about ourselves. We begin to think we have grown all we are going to grow, that there is nothing new or fascinating to know about ourselves. We think there are no new regions to explore or that change is no longer possible. But the Apostle Paul reminds us that we can always experience spiritual growth. He wrote, "Even though our physical being is gradually decaying, yet our spiritual being is renewed day after day" (2 Corinthians 4:16 GNT).

Likewise, Jael's story shows us that God has more resources at His disposal than we can ever begin to see. When we thought Deborah was going to be the hero, somewhere out at a campsite, not an Israelite or Canaanite campsite, God had another woman waiting. Whatever Jael's motives were, however much commentators may be critical of her, the Book of Judges shows her to be a hero—God's hero.

God doesn't always work predictably or obviously, and this knowledge should encourage us when our vision is limited. I remember when this realization hit home with me. My husband, a college administrator, had experienced some job difficulties so bizarre that finding another job was *appearing* to be impossible. I remember sitting in Sunday School one winter Sunday morning and realizing through the lesson being taught that I was only considering the dimension I could see—what was around us and what Bob and I could do. I remembered being encouraged that day as I realized I was forgetting that God had resources far beyond what I could see.

In March, I received a phone call. It was from a pastor in another state, someone we knew but not well. Our paths had crossed earlier when he had been on a church staff where we worshipped. He had moved on and we had left that church. We didn't keep in regular contact; we didn't even exchange Christmas cards.

The previous Sunday, Bill explained to me, he had been absent from his pulpit and had asked a Christian college president to fill in for him. When Bill returned to his office, he played the tape of the president's message. The president had said the college was looking for people to fill two administrative positions they had open.

Through some mutual friends Bill had learned Bob was unemployed. After listening to the tape, Bill called us. He said to me, "I think this is it," meaning this will be the spot for Bob. I knew it, too. It was as if God himself had called, and even though Bob had to apply and interview for the job, I knew deep within my bones that this would be Bob's next job, and it was. During those early winter days, when I had tried to figure out what was next, or even if there would be a next, it never occurred to me to think about Bill as being a conduit for God to work. He was out of my view, but not out of God's.

God always has more resources than we can see or realize. Through a tent-dwelling woman God subdued Jabin and God's people lived without oppression for the next 40 years. Through a pastor in another state He rescued our livelihood, helping me to always remember that He "is able to do so much more than we can ever ask for, or even think of" (Ephesians 3:20 GNT). To God be the glory!

Becoming a *wonder* woman

Of what good is it to study the life of someone whom we might not want to emulate?

How do you evaluate Jael as a *wonder* woman? Should she be on the list or not be on the list?

What did Jael do right? What did Jael do wrong?

What did Sisera assume about Jael?

What can be wrong with assumptions?

When has God acted counter to how you thought He was going to act? Was that unsettling or encouraging to you?

Chapter Eleven

ABIGAIL

You Did That? Without Your Husband Knowing?

1 Samuel 25; 27:3; 30:3, 5, 18;
2 Samuel 2:2; 3:3; 1 Chronicles 3:1

When I asked a woman whose husband was a PhD candidate how he was doing, she began to cry. Tears trickled down her cheeks as she said, "He has almost completed all the requirements, but he is throwing in the towel. We've reserved a U-Haul truck for this weekend. We're moving back home."

"Doesn't this upset you after all the sacrifices you have made?"

"Well, yes, it does," she answered, "but I can't say anything to him."

"Why not?"

"Because of Ephesians 5:22."

"You mean the apostle Paul's words about being a submissive wife?"

"Yes, it wouldn't be right for me to tell him what to do."

I thought of my own husband's hard work to get a doctorate in education. Sure, there were discouraging times, but if he had gotten near the end and wanted to quit, I would have said something to him. I was a submissive wife, and I am a submissive wife, but there are times when for the good of everyone you have to take action, just as Abigail did.

Who was Abigail?

Abigail was a beautiful, intelligent woman who was married to Nabal, a man whose name means "fool." He was a mean and churlish man, while she "was a woman of good understanding and beautiful appearance" (1 Samuel 25:3 NKJV).

They lived during the time when Saul was king of God's people, albeit in name only. He had disobeyed God, so the prophet Samuel had anointed David, the son of Jesse, to be the next king. Saul, though, didn't want to give up his role and he determined to get rid of David. He earnestly pursued David with the intent of killing him.

Needing protection from Saul and wanting to build his power base, David gathered a group of misfits around him. Naturally, they took to the wilderness areas. While they lived an outlaw existence in the sense that they were running from authority, they did not behave like outlaws. They did good things for the people in whose areas they were hiding. They protected people and their flocks from roving bands of robbers. There weren't any formal arrangements with the locals about this protection; it was just done. Still, David assumed, as Rahab had, that one good turn deserves another.

When David and his men were hiding out in the wilderness of Paran, they guarded Nabal's flocks and protected his shepherds. Nabal was a wealthy rancher.

He ". . . had three thousand sheep and a thousand goats" (1 Samuel 25:2 NKJV). They did this night and day; David's men ". . . were a wall" around the shepherds, sheep, and goats (1 Samuel 25:16 NKJV).

When the time came for the annual shearing of sheep in Carmel where Nabal's property was located. David knew there would be feasting along with the shearing. It was a time of work and celebration. In David's mind, it was payback time. He hoped to share in the food that would be a major part of the celebration so he sent ten of his young men to where Nabal was shearing his sheep. He gave them these instructions:

> "Go up to Carmel, go to Nabal, and greet him in my name. And thus you shall say to him who lives in prosperity: 'Peace be to you, peace to your house, and peace to all that you have! . . . Your shepherds were with us, and we did not hurt them, nor was there anything missing from them all the while they were in Carmel. Ask your young men, and they will tell you. Therefore let my young men find favor in your eyes, for we come on a feast day. Please give whatever comes to your hand to your servants and to your son David'" (1 Samuel 25:5–6, 7–8 NKJV).

But Nabal didn't see the situation the same way David did.

Nabal's response

David's young men did exactly as they were told and waited for his response. It wasn't what they expected to hear.

Nabal said, "Who is David, and who is the son of Jesse? There are many servants nowadays who break away each one from his master. Shall I then take my bread and my water and my meat that I have killed for my shearers, and give it to men when I do not know where they are from?" (1 Samuel 25:10–11 NKJV).

Taken aback, David's young men turned on their heels and left. They hurried back to David and told him what Nabal had said. What? This man is not going to give us any food after what we have done for him? David didn't say this, but he was sure thinking it. He was angry and Nabal would pay!

"Then David said to his men, 'Every man gird on his sword.' So every man girded on his sword and David also girded on his sword. And about four hundred men went with David, and two hundred stayed with the supplies" (1 Samuel 25:12–13 NKJV).

Nabal, of course, back at his place, was blissfully unaware of the effect his words and refusal had had on David. He was totally into the shearing event, where much food was being served and liquor was flowing. He didn't sense any kind of danger. One of his workers did, though, and knew they were in big trouble. He was alarmed and hurried to tell Abigail what was happening.

There's going to be trouble

Sensing impending disaster from Nabal's reaction to David's request, the young worker said to Abigail, "Look, David sent messengers from the wilderness to greet our master; and he reviled them" (1 Samuel 25:14–17 NKJV).

He assured her that David and his men had been good to them; they deserved better treatment. "But the men were very good to us, and we were not hurt, nor did we miss anything as long as we accompanied them, when we were in the fields. They were a wall to us both by night and day, all the time we were with them keeping the sheep" (1 Samuel 25:15–17 NKJV).

He didn't tell her what to do—he was a servant—but he asked her to think about and consider the situation. And then he stated the awful consequences if something weren't done. "Now therefore, know and consider what you will do, for harm is determined against our master and against all his household" (1 Samuel 25:17 NKJV). If David wasn't stopped, Nabal was going to be hurt and so was everyone associated with him. Many innocent people were going to suffer as a result of Nabal's actions. The servant was quite blunt about why he didn't approach Nabal. He said, "He is such a scoundrel that one cannot speak to him" (1 Samuel 25:17 NKJV). Do you get the impression that Nabal had behaved similarly before?

Abigail quickly appraised the situation and agreed that something needed to be done and done immediately. She hurriedly prepared generous gifts for David and his men: 200 loaves of bread, two skins of wine, five sheep already dressed, a bushel of roasted grain, 100 clusters of raisins, and 200 cakes of figs. I marvel that this much food could be gathered *quickly!* Perhaps this was part of the food ready for the feast Nabal was giving. If not, gathering these supplies certainly puts her in the *wonder* woman category.

All the food gifts were loaded on donkeys, and the servants were sent on ahead with the gifts to intercept David and his men as they headed toward Carmel. Abigail said, "You go on, I will come after you." Then she left, and the Bible specifically says, "But she did not tell her husband Nabal" (1 Samuel 25:19 NKJV).

She went off with servants to meet 400 men and she didn't tell Nabal she was going. She took food and gifts from her husband's household—food that her husband had worked hard to produce and she didn't tell him about it.

You've got to be kidding! What was she thinking?

Wonder woman's wisdom

Abigail was wise to act immediately. She knew Nabal's insult was so great that David would be very angry, and he was. David did not stop to think about who might be innocent and who might be guilty. He and his men planned to kill all the males of Nabal's household. There was nothing rational about his behavior.

Abigail, in an effort to save innocent lives, bravely went to meet 400 angry men armed with swords. That alone makes her a *wonder* woman, but what she did when she saw David makes her a *wise wonder* woman.

"As she came riding her donkey into a mountain ravine, there were David and his men descending toward her" (1 Samuel 25:20 NIV). David was still smarting from Nabal's disregard for his protection and for repaying his goodness with evil. He had just said to his men, "May God deal with David, be it ever so severely, if by morning I leave alive one male of all who belong to him!" (1 Samuel 25:22 NIV).

What Abigail did next shows both wisdom and courage, and we can learn a lot from Abigail about defusing a volatile situation.

- *She was humble.* Abigail dismounted quickly from the donkey when she saw David. She fell on her face before him and bowed down to the ground. Even though she was a woman of high socioeconomic status by virtue of her rich husband, and David was an outlaw on the run, she referred to David as "my lord" and to herself as "your maidservant."
- *She accepted responsibility for what happened.* "She fell at [David's] feet and said: 'On me, my lord, on me let this iniquity be!'" (1 Samuel 25:24 NKJV). She went on to say that she had not seen his men when they came to her house; the implication was if she had, she surely would have done something about it. She would have given them food.
- *She asked for forgiveness.* "And now this present which your maidservant has brought to my lord, let it be given to the young men who follow my lord. Please forgive the trespass of your maidservant" (1 Samuel 25:27-28a NKJV). Even though she was not guilty, she offered an apology, and an apology is a great ointment to pour on any wound. It has wonderful healing power.
- *She excused Nabal.* She didn't ignore Nabal's part in the situation, but she represented her husband in a light way without being disrespectful to him. She said, in essence, "You've got to understand, God love him, sometimes my husband makes mistakes. What can I say? He lives up to his name!"
- *She saw herself as God's servant.* Abigail's wisdom allowed her to understand the danger of the situation and to recognize many innocent lives would be lost, but her wisdom is even more impressive when you

> realize she could see the long-range consequences for David, too. She realized that going to meet David—stopping David in his tracks—was God's way of stopping him from doing something he would later regret. She assured him that he was indeed God's anointed for king, and that God was going to protect him and take care of his enemies. He didn't need to kill without cause or take revenge. "Don't kill today and you won't have on your conscience remorse for having taken revenge and killed without cause."

Abigail was indeed God's servant to David, for when he heard what she had to say, he knew she was right. His anger dissipated, and disaster was averted.

David's response

David was relieved and happy about Abigail's running interference and speaking with him. "David said to Abigail: 'Blessed is the LORD God of Israel, who sent you this day to meet me! And blessed is your advice and blessed are you, because you have kept me this day from coming to bloodshed and from avenging myself with my own hand. For indeed, as the LORD God of Israel lives, who has kept me back from hurting you, unless you had hurried and come to meet me, surely by morning light no males would have been left to Nabal!'" (1 Samuel 25:32–34 NKJV).

David accepted her gifts and said to her, "Go home in peace. I have heard your words and granted your request" (1 Samuel 25:35 NIV).

What tension! What drama! What resolution! And Nabal had no idea. At home, he was unaware that his life was in danger. He was holding a feast and having a great time while Abigail was saving his life.

When she got back home, she found Nabal drunk. She decided to wait until morning to tell him when he was sober. The news was too much for him. The Bible says "his heart died within him, and he became like a stone" (1 Samuel 25:37 NKJV), which means he probably had a stroke. Ten days later, he died.

David saw his death as the hand of God. He said, "Praise the LORD! He has taken revenge on Nabal for insulting me and has kept me his servant from doing wrong. The LORD has punished Nabal for his evil" (1 Samuel 25:39 GNT).

David also saw these events as an opportunity to gain an intelligent, beautiful wife. He wooed Abigail through his servants as was proper and she agreed to marry him. With the same quick assessment of the situation and the same humility that she exemplified earlier, she responded again. "Then she arose, bowed her face to the earth, and said, 'Here is your maidservant, a servant to wash the feet of the servants of my lord.' So Abigail rose in haste and rode on a donkey, attended by five of her maidens; and she followed the messengers of David, and became his wife" (1 Samuel 25:41–42 NKJV).

Lassoing Abigail

What do we learn from Abigail? That married women don't have to be submissive wives? No, sorry!

What we can learn from her is that being submissive

does not mean being blind, and this is something all women, whether married or single, need to be aware of. Submission is a Christian principle, a way for living and working together harmoniously, and most of us are in submission to someone. It could be a spouse, a boss, a parent, a pastor or organizational leader. In the Christian family, we are to be submitting to one another (Ephesians 5:21).

When we submit, we surrender our will to someone else's, but that other person is not perfect. He or she could have an off day, make a mistake, or fail to see the ramifications of his or her decisions. Or he or she could be "dense" like Nabal and just not pick up on what is really happening. We all have times like that (although Nabal seemed to have a reputation for them), and that's when we need an Abigail in our life to pick up the slack, remind us of what we are doing wrong, or help us see the folly of our ways.

Is a spouse always right?

Is a parent always correct?

Does a boss never make mistakes?

Is a pastor's judgment never faulty?

Most of the mistakes people in direct authority over us make are ones we can overlook because they don't do any real damage, but when a mistake is going to have wide-ranging consequences, such as Nabal's and David's, then a wise woman speaks up. She is tactful, she is humble, she is apologetic—but she speaks up because it is the right thing to do.

The intent is never to embarrass the person in authority, put him or her down, be critical, or usurp the person's position. The motive is to be as pure as Abigail's was. She was certain that God was leading her. That's the key for us right there. When God puts it on our heart to speak to someone in authority, then that's the time to do it.

Many readers may not agree with me about this. I understand. I just know I love my husband enough that if he were making a serious mistake, I would speak up. For example, if he had gotten close to completing his doctorate degree and was ready to quit, I would have questioned him. I would have put my arms lovingly around Bob and said, "Honey, I know this has been tough, but try to hang in there. Let's talk about it and see if there are any solutions we are overlooking. Let's pray about it together and ask God to lead us." That's the lesson Abigail teaches me.

Becoming a *wonder* woman

Abigail is described as "good in understanding." What does that mean? Is that why the servant went to her instead of to Nabal?

What does the way Abigail approached David and what she said to him say about her?

Was Abigail God's instrument in holding David back from killing Nabal's men or was she simply a shrewd woman?

From what spiritual consequences did Abigail's words save David?

Do the words about submission in Ephesians 5 mean a wife must always allow her husband to make all the decisions?

Who has been an Abigail in your life? What wise woman kept you from doing something you would later regret?

Chapter Twelve

THE WISE WOMAN OF ABEL

You Threw Whose Head?

2 Samuel 20:1–23

This *wonder* woman story takes place during the time of David, although at a later time than Abigail's story. David had been king long enough for his throne to be challenged. One of his sons, Absalom, had even tried to defeat David and gain the throne. Through shrewd political maneuvering, Absalom gained the people's favor and attempted to overthrow his father. Joab, David's military commander, had squelched this rebellion and had seen to it that Absalom was killed. While technically David still possessed the throne, he had the challenge of regaining the support of the people. "Even though David was the Lord's anointed, the political affairs of the nation still had to be dealt with in very human ways."[1]

A worthless fellow and somewhat of a hothead by the name of Sheba urged the northerners of David's kingdom not to support him. Unlike Absalom, Sheba did not attack

David or attempt to replace him as king; he stirred up trouble and raised the level of discontent at a time when David needed unity. Sheba's words were effective, convincing the northerners that they had nothing to gain from following David. Only Judah, in the south, remained loyal and supportive of David.

A king could not allow this kind of talk and behavior to continue, so David instructed his military leader and his servants to pursue Sheba. Others joined the pursuit along the way. As David's group gathered forces, so did Sheba. He gathered his kinsmen and fled far north to the city of Abel Beth Maacah, to the periphery of David's kingdom. With David's men hot in pursuit, Sheba hid out in this fortified city.

A fortified city was a walled city, like Jericho was when Rahab had assisted God's people. Big, thick, high walls surrounded it. The walls had gates that could be opened during the day for people to come and go, but they were closed at night or any time when danger threatened. After Sheba arrived, the city closed its gates and waited apprehensively. This was exactly what David was afraid would occur. Sheba would hole up in a fortified city, and his men would not be able to get him. What would happen next?

A city under siege

By the time David's men arrived at Abel Beth Maacah, Joab was in charge of the troops. Determined to get Sheba, they immediately began a siege of the city. Joab's men heard that Sheba was there, and so they went and besieged the city. They built ramps of earth against the outer wall, so they could use battering rams. (If you recall from chapter 1 of this book, there were usually two walls around a fortified city.) They also began to dig under the wall to make it fall down. No depending on silently marching seven times around the city to be victorious this time!

As some city residents perched on top of the walls and looked down, they were disturbed and frightened by what they saw. What was going on? Why were these men trying to destroy their walls? They needed their walls, and besides, they were a peaceful community. They were known for being peaceful and faithful to God. People came for miles to find answers at Abel Beth Maacah. Engaging in battle was a foreign concept to them. Who were these people now attacking their city? They recognized Joab and realized the army must be David's men, but why? And what would happen if they broke down the walls and entered the city? Would fighting follow? How many innocent people were going to suffer? Would people be killed?

As residents talked and wrung their hands, one of them took action. There was a woman among them who said, "Enough is enough!"

The Bible doesn't tell us much about her—doesn't even give her a name—but it does call her "wise" (2 Samuel 20:16a NIV). She valued her city and knew someone needed to defend it, or at least investigate to see what all the fuss was about. She went to the wall and shouted.

"Listen! Listen! Tell Joab to come here; I want to speak with him." Joab went, and she asked, "Are you Joab?"

"'Yes, I am," he answered.

"Listen to me, sir," she said to him.

"'I'm listening," he answered.

The woman said, "Long ago they used to say, 'Go and get your answer in the city of Abel'—and that's just what they did. Ours is a great city, one of the most peaceful and loyal in Israel. Why are you trying to destroy it? Do you want to ruin what belongs to the Lord?" (2 Samuel 20:16–19 GNT).

If any question would make you stop and assess what you were doing, this one would: "Do you want to ruin what belongs to the Lord?" That one would make you see what you were doing in a whole different light! She accused Joab of waging a war of conquest against his own people, the Lord's own heritage. Joab realized "the folly of shedding the innocent blood of the inhabitants of Abel, thus creating another incident which would make the pacification of Israel still more difficult."[2]

Joab, who had been so intent on getting Sheba that he hadn't considered what the consequences would be for Abel, reframed his intent in answering her. Joab said, "I will never ruin or destroy your city! That is not our plan. A man named Sheba started a rebellion against King David. Hand him over, and I will withdraw my men from this city."

She quickly analyzed the situation. To spare innocent citizens from slaughter and their city walls from being destroyed, she said, "We will throw Sheba's head over the wall to you."

Then she went to the people of the city with her plan. The townspeople's reaction to her plan reveals their respect for her. They might have chosen not to listen to her. Their response might have been, "What are you thinking? You want us to find Sheba, cut off his head and throw it across the walls to Joab? You've got to be kidding. Woman, there are battering rams out there and the men are digging furiously. It is just a matter of time until we will all be dead."

But they didn't react this way. They respected her and they recognized the wisdom in her solution, even if it seems gruesome to us.

"They cut off Sheba's head and threw it over the wall to Joab. He blew the trumpet as a signal for his men to leave the city, and they went back home. And Joab returned to Jerusalem to the king" (2 Samuel 20:22 GNT).

Through a woman's intervention, a city was spared from ruin and many lives were saved. No doubt about it, she deserves the title, The *Wise* Woman of Abel. What is it that makes this woman wise?

A wise woman's wisdom

Wisdom is not the same as knowledge. Knowledge applies to any body of facts gathered by study, observation, or similar means, and to the ideas inferred from these facts; it also connotes an understanding of what is known, as opposed to being able to recite facts just for facts' sake. Wisdom includes knowledge—a knowledge of people, life and conduct, but the facts are so thoroughly assimilated that sound judgment, insight and mental discernment are produced. We can better understand wisdom when we analyze what the Wise Woman of Abel did.

- *She investigated.* Wisdom seeks knowledge. The Wise Woman of Abel gathered the facts. She was the one person in that town who was willing to check out the scene of conflict. Others stood on the wall and saw what was happening, and their fears escalated. She looked fear in the face and went to the scene to find out what was really going on. A wise person looks at the facts.

  In her investigation, the first thing she did was to make sure she was talking to the person in charge. From the walls, it would have been easy for the people to speculate and to assume Joab was behind the siege. The first thing she did was to call out, "Tell Joab to come here so I can speak to him" (2 Samuel 20:16 NIV) and then she said, "Are you Joab?" (2 Samuel 20:17 NIV). She was going to get the facts right.

- *She was courageous*. You have to wonder if she was aware of Joab's reputation. If she was, she was a mighty brave woman.

  Joab was a man used to shedding blood. Whatever Joab wanted, Joab got. Although Joab was loyal to David, he was also ruthless in looking after his and David's interests. He treacherously murdered Abner, an early rival to David's being king. He murdered Absalom, David's son, the one who wanted to replace David. Joab plunged 3 darts in him. He murdered Amasa, a rival of his, on the way to Abel in pursuit of Sheba. He reached out to Amasa as if to embrace him and then disemboweled Amasa with one stroke of his sword. And she said to this man, "Listen to me, sir!" (2 Samuel 20:17 GNT). This was one confident, strong woman.
- *She reasoned.* As she talked with Joab, she made a quick mental appraisal. Why should innocent people die defending the life of a hothead who wants to undermine the king? If we turn Sheba over to Joab, he will die. If we don't turn him over, Joab's forces will tear down our walls, come in, and kill Sheba, and possibly many others, as well. Either way, Sheba will die. There seemed to be one reasonable solution, if it were gross and that was get rid of Sheba.
- *She was decisive*. She assessed the options and recommended the soundest course of action based on her perception and understanding.

A wise person has this kind of ability. She and Abigail were alike in this regard. When Nabal's servant went to Abigail with the news of her husband's cavalier treatment of David, Abigail immediately sized up the situation and knew how to defuse David's anger.

Some people can assess a situation and even see what needs to be done, but are hesitant to say anything. They don't have confidence in themselves or in God; they fear they will be wrong, of that people won't like them.

- *She saw the big picture*. In their assessments, both Abigail and the Wise Woman of Abel both saw the greater good. They both acted on behalf of others. The women could have hidden themselves and gone into a self-protective mode, thinking only of themselves. But these two women saw the harm that could come to others—Abigail thought of her husband and their many servants and the Wise Woman of Abel thought of the city and the nation.
- *She was direct with Joab*. There was no coy approach on the part of the Wise Woman of Abel. She spoke with the authority that comes from wisdom, with the confidence that this is the right approach for the community of Abel, for King David, and for God. She asked, "Why do you want to swallow up the Lord's inheritance?" (2 Samuel 20:19 NIV). In other words, "Joab, are you going to work against God himself by destroying His people?"
- *She consulted with the townspeople*. She also spoke directly with the city residents. She didn't try to single-handedly play the part of Town Hero and save the town. She

enlisted the help of her fellow citizens. Wise people seek the input and cooperation of others.
- "The philosophy of the Wise Woman of Abel was an admirable one: ascertain the real cause of the dispute and then see to it that the real nature of that real cause is thoroughly understood by the common people . . . The wise woman was never so wise as when she told the people the truth."[3]

Within every man and woman is the potential to be wise, and yet not all people become wise. Wisdom is often associated with older people—and experience seems to be necessary to develop the kind of reasoning associated with wisdom—but not all old people are wise. Some of them make some very foolish decisions. So is there anything a woman can do to become wiser or is it just a gift that some people have?

When you want to be wiser

The Bible makes it clear that wisdom is a gift God wants to give men and women who seek it; it is not something bestowed on a select few. Here are some things a woman can do if she wants to pursue wisdom.

- *Pray*. Through prayer, we can open ourselves to receive wisdom by asking God for it. The Bible says, "If any of you lack wisdom, let him ask of God, that giveth to all men liberally, and upbraideth not; and it shall be given him" (James 1:5 KJV).
- *Increase knowledge*. "The fear of the LORD is the beginning of knowledge; but fools despise wisdom

and instruction" (Proverbs 1:7 KJV). While knowledge and wisdom aren't synonymous, increasing your knowledge will contribute to the growth of wisdom in your life, particularly biblical knowledge. When we gain knowledge, when we exercise our mind, and learn, our base of making discernment is broadened and strengthened.

- *Live the way God wants you to live*. A ministry friend of mine is often sought out by people for her counsel. The question she learned to ask was, Do you want God's wisdom? She had found through past experience that people often came to her just to vent, to have their interpretations of their situation underscored, or to have their feelings validated. They really weren't interested in God's wisdom. To become wise, we want and need to apply God's wisdom to our living, and insight about Him and about life will come to us as a result. The Bible says, "Keep my commandments, and live; and my law as the apple of thine eye. Bind them upon thy fingers, write them upon the table of thine heart. Say unto wisdom, Thou art my sister; and call understanding thy kinswoman" (Proverbs 7:2–4 KJV).
- *Try to get the big picture*. By the way our brains are wired, women are prone to being detail specialists, which is a pretty good specialty to have unless you become too caught up in the details. We may see so many details we never get the big picture. One way we can break ourselves of this is by asking questions like these: What are the long-range consequences? Who else besides me will be affected by the outcome? How will they be affected? What's God view? How is He seeing this? What is His perspective?

- *Aim for an objective picture*. Another help in getting the big picture is striving for a less personal picture. Some women take things too personally to be wise. They can't seem to step outside of themselves or of their situation and see how others might be affected.
- *Become more decisive*. Abigail, Deborah, and the Wise Woman of Abel were all decisive women. To be like them, we may have to make a wrong decision here and there along the way. Otherwise we stay in the land of indecisiveness. God is the redeemer of any faulty decision, but we can learn about ourselves and about life by being definitive even if we are sometimes wrong.
- *Associate with wise people*. The Wise Woman of Abel lived among wise people. Sometimes we can be around people who can talk a subject to death, be too negative, never get beyond their own feelings, or never try to see things from another's perspective. If these are the only kind of people we associate with, our thinking will be similar to theirs. Look around. Who are the wise women you know? Have you hung out with them lately? "He who walks with the wise grows wise, but a companion of fools suffers harm" (Proverbs 13:20 NIV).

This list spells out just some of the things a woman can do if she wants to pursue wisdom. I hope the stories of Deborah, Abigail and the Wise Woman of Abel will encourage you to do that. We never know when we are going to be in a situation that will call for an astute appraisal, an ability to see a solution, and a decisiveness to act. I want to be ready. Don't you?

Becoming a *wonder* woman

What is wisdom?

How are age and wisdom related?

How were the wisdom of Abigail and the wisdom of Wise Woman of Abel alike?

Who are the wisest women you know? What have you observed about them that made you conclude they are wise?

Do you anticipate growing wiser? How can you assure this will happen?

If only one word could describe you (as the word *wise* described the wise woman of Abel), what would you want that word to be?

Chapter Thirteen

THE SYROPHOENICIAN WOMAN

The Nerve!

Matthew 15:21–28; Mark 7:24–30

Have you ever felt the frustration of needing some time alone and finding it almost impossible to get? You have a job that needs to be completed, a job that calls for focus. You need to be left alone, but someone leans over the cubicle with numerous questions about his or her project. You crave some time by yourself so that you can renew your spirit. Finally the day arrives when you have no appointments, you fix yourself a cup of tea, open your Bible and the phone rings. It's the school nurse; your child is sick with a fever; can you come and get her? You plan for a Friday night at home alone with your spouse and the door bell rings. You open the door to find your adult kids. "Surprise!" If you identify with any of these scenarios, you can understand what Jesus experienced when He tried to find time to be alone.

Plans interrupted

After a year into His ministry, Jesus became very popular. Wherever he went throughout Palestine, and especially in Galilee, immense crowds followed Him. Consequently opposition and suspicion developed against Him. The religious leaders from Jerusalem infiltrated the crowds and raised questions to try to discredit Him in front of the people. They didn't like what He was saying and how He was influencing the people. Herod Antipas, the governor of Galilee, worried that Jesus, with such a large following, could become a political threat, so he had Him watched. Some people were already thinking Jesus might possibly be the Messiah. Some actually referred to Him as "the son of David." Herod worried that Jesus might start an uprising. Aware of the mounting opposition, Jesus realized that His time was limited. He needed to teach His followers so they could carry on His message after He was gone. To do this, He attempted to withdraw from the crowds for uninterrupted time with His disciples.

His popularity made withdrawal with His disciples really hard. His first attempt failed. They had left Galilee, crossed the lake by boat, and gone to eastern Palestine. But when they got across the lake, the people—the very ones they had tried to escape—were waiting for them! When Jesus and His disciples rowed back across the lake, there they were again. Out of compassion, Jesus fed these people. Seeing what He could do, the people wanted to make Him their political leader (John 6:14–15), and the religious leaders increased their harassment. Now it was even more imperative that the disciples understand His true mission so He tried again to get away with them.

This time, Jesus and His disciples headed to Gentile territory, out from Herod Antipas's jurisdiction, where people didn't know Him and the Jewish religious leaders would not be present. They went to the territory of Tyre and Sidon, where old Phoenicia used to be. Hopefully, in this Gentile area, they would be undisturbed. To make sure, they went inside a house, assuming the walls and closed door would hide them from the crowds, but "he could not be hid" (Mark 7:24 KJV). He could not keep His presence secret.

Evidently stories about Jesus and His miracle-working abilities had spread to Gentile country. Once someone spotted Him, word spread and people gathered around the house. One person, bolder than the others, pushed her way through the crowd and into the house. She was not only an interruption to Jesus's plans, her behavior was uncouth and rowdy. She was a wild woman, someone you wouldn't suspect of being a *wonder* woman, but she was.

A determined mother

The Bible describes this woman as a Syrophoenician, a Greek, and a Canaanite. Tyre and Sidon were in Syria where ancient Phoenicia had been, hence, she's called the Syrophoenician woman. She spoke Greek, as most people throughout the Roman Empire did, so Mark referred to her as Greek (Mark 7:26*a* NIV). Matthew—he wrote for Jews—called her a Canaanite (Matthew 15:22*a* NIV), linking her with those who occupied the Promised Land when it was promised to Abraham many years earlier. The descendants of the Canaanites were often spoken of with reproach in the Old Testament. By mentioning that she was a Canaanite, Matthew was building drama into the story. He was letting the reader know that, of all people, she was someone who should not have been approaching a Jew for help, but she did. She sought Jesus's help. She was a determined mother who wanted help for her daughter who was "suffering terribly from demon-possession" (Matthew 15:22 NIV).

With so brief of a description, it is hard to know what the daughter's symptoms were. Various mental, emotional and physical disturbances were attributed to demons, evil spirits, or unclean spirits. In some people, their sight and speech were affected. "Some people brought to Jesus a man who was blind and could not talk because he had a demon" (Matthew 12:22*a* GNT). Others who were possessed spoke audibly but strangely. Some afflicted screamed (Mark 1:26; 5:5 GNT).

Strange behavior was also characteristic of the demon possessed. The Gerasene demonic "wandered among the tombs and through the hills, screaming and cutting himself with stones" (Mark 5:5 GNT). A boy possessed by an evil spirit foamed at the mouth, gritted his teeth, and became stiff all over (Mark 9:18*a* GNT). One boy had such terrible attacks that he often fell in the fire or into water (Matthew 17:15 GNT).

No wonder the Syrophoenician woman wanted help for her daughter, who was suffering terribly. Perhaps she had already sought help from the exorcists in her area. Exorcists were prevalent because there was such a pervasive belief in demons. They used elaborate incantations, spells, and magical rites to drive out demons. That's why the people in Capernaum of Galilee were impressed with Jesus; earlier in His ministry Jesus exorcised a demon from a man with a word of clear, simple, brief authority (Mark 1:23–27 GNT). No one had seen anything like it!

Perhaps this was one of the stories about Jesus that fanned out into Gentile country. The Syrophenician woman had perhaps heard the story, and hope had leaped within her! When she heard Jesus was in the area, she started looking for Him. Deep within her mother's heart, she knew He could set her daughter free, if she could just get to Him! It wasn't going to be easy, but she was determined.

She pushed her way through the crowds and through the door. Over and over she loudly cried out, "Have mercy on me, O Lord, thou Son of David, my daughter is grievously vexed with a devil" (Matthew 15:22 KJV). She had heard the rumors that He was the Jewish Messiah, and to get help for her daughter, she was willing to acknowledge this even though she wasn't Jewish. She acknowledged Him, but He didn't acknowledge her, at least not right away.

Jesus's initial response

Jesus was aware of the commotion and of her noisy entrance. He could hear her loud cries, but He didn't say anything (Matthew 15:23*a* KJV), and we wish He would. It just seems so unlike Jesus to not respond immediately to a mother's request, but Jesus wasn't always quick to respond (John 8:4–9; 11:5–6; Matthew 27:11–14). Sometimes His response required a weighing of the situation.

In this instance, perhaps He was prayerfully discerning the best course of action. Who is this woman? Is she here to make a scene to prove some kind of point or is she really sincere? Could her request be a trap or a trick as the religious leaders questions were? What if I stop and help this woman who is interrupting our getaway time? If I heal her daughter, will many people come seeking help as they did when I set the demon possessed man free at Capernaum and healed Simon Peter's mother-in-law? (Mark 1:29–31). Is this what the Father wants? Is the time ripe for ministry to the Gentiles? Or should I ignore her and stay focused on my purpose for being here?

While Jesus pondered what to do, His disciples didn't have any trouble deciding. They urged Jesus to give her whatever she wanted. They said, "Send her away, for she keeps crying out after us" (Matthew 15:23 NIV). Unlike their Teacher, they were not thinking of long-range consequences, nor were they responding out of compassion. They regarded her as a nuisance. This Gentile woman had come unbidden into the house; she hadn't been invited. She had no right to expect help from a Jew. Actually she had no right to even be speaking directly to Jewish males. She should have had her husband or father or brother to intercede on her behalf. She hadn't been invited to be a part of their meeting, so their attitude was, Give her what she wants, so we can get rid of her.

When they spoke, Jesus broke His silence. He looked at the disciples and said, "I was sent only to the lost sheep of Israel" (Matthew 15:24 NIV). They knew by His reference to "the lost sheep of Israel," He meant the Jews. In effect, He was asking, "So you think I should only minister to Jews? Do you want me to focus only on people like ourselves?"[1]

In the small house, the woman heard what Jesus said, and she could have been discouraged by his statement. She had no reason to think that Jesus, a Jew, would listen to a Canaanite, but she was determined. Her daughter's life was at stake, and she had the audacious hope to believe that Jesus was her answer. She pressed on. She fell down before Jesus and said, "Lord, help me!"

Realizing she had heard the comment He had made about Jews to the disciples and that she still was not discouraged, He continued the thought with her. "First let the children eat all they want," he told her, "for it is not right to take the children's bread and toss it to their dogs" (Mark 7:27 NIV). Obviously, the "children" referred to the Jews; her people were the "dogs." He wasn't calling her a dog; he was simply speaking in the ordinary parlance of the day. The Jews had contempt for Gentiles, and the Gentiles felt the same way about them. He softened the effect by using the Aramaic word for puppy and not the word for street dogs. "There were two different Aramaic words for 'dog.' *Pariah* were the wild, often rabid, street dogs that everyone feared and avoided, and *kunaria* were the cute, cuddly puppy dogs people kept in their homes. Jesus used the more familiar and friendlier term."[2]

Nevertheless, He was implying that the salvation He offered was to Jews first and then eventually to the Gentiles (which is how the gospel unfolds in the New Testament). Basically He was saying, "Your day will come."

Jesus, as always, knew what He was doing. He set aside His agenda and gave her the opportunity to show her true colors. Would she catch the significance of His words? How would she respond? Would she continue in her persistence? Just how brave was she?

She picked up on His choice of words, and used them in her counterargument. Yes, counterargument. This woman had the nerve to challenge Jesus.

Her shining moment

When Jesus said, "It is not right to take the children's bread and toss it to their dogs," the woman immediately replied, "Yes, Lord, but even the dogs under the table eat the children's crumbs" (Mark 7:28 NIV). She made a valid point.

According to Dwight L. Moody, she was saying something like this: "'Yes, Lord, I acknowledge I am a Gentile dog; but I remember that even the dogs have some privileges, and when the door is open they slink in and crawl under the table. When the bread or the meat sifts through the cracks of the table or falls off the edge of it, they pick it up, and the master of the house is not angry with them. I do not ask for a big loaf; I do not ask even for a big slice; I only ask for that which drops down through the chinks of the table—the dogs' portion. I ask only the crumbs.'"[3]

Jesus was not shocked or put off by her answer. He loved it. (Notice the exclamation mark in Matthew 15:28.) "Jesus was master of retort,"[4] and He appreciated her quick reply. He was aware that she was familiar with His reputation as a miracle worker, a possible political Messiah, an authoritative teacher, and an exorcist, and yet she was not afraid to converse with Him. (While we may be aghast that she would actually challenge Jesus, we must remember that He was not God to her. She knew him as a healer and an exorcist.)

She didn't answer Jesus to show Him up, to embarrass Him, or to demonstrate how smart she was. Her reply was born out of love. She was propelled to persevere and to speak up because she was a mother seeking help for her daughter.

Her answer exuded faith. "OK, Lord, I acknowledge that Jews should come first and salvation will be later for the Gentiles, but you can throw me some crumbs now."

Her ability to think and respond so nimbly makes her faith all the more remarkable. Thinking can increase our energy, encourage creativity, and invigorate the soul but thinking can also turn a person into a cynic or a skeptic. A thinker's flame of faith can be fanned by recognizing possibilities and seeing alternatives that non-thinkers may never see, but thinking can also cause us to be so rational that it discourages faith. If the Syrophoenician woman had taken a rational approach, she would have considered the circumstances that she was a Gentile and Jesus was a Jew and wouldn't even have approached Him. Logic would have said no Jew would help a Gentile woman.

But her thinking was alive with the possibility that Jesus could heal her daughter even if her daughter was not present. It is one thing to hear about someone who can perform miracles; it is another thing to act on that faith. Faith gave her the courage to pursue help for her daughter. It was faith that would not take "no" for an answer, and it was rewarded.

Her answer brought joy to Christ in a trying time, and it gave Him the opportunity to minister to her. He told her, "For such a reply you will get what you are seeking. Woman, you have great faith! Go home now; the demon has left your daughter" (author's paraphrase of Mark 7:29 and Matthew 15:28). "She went home and found her child lying on the bed, and the demon gone" (Mark 7:30 NIV).

Jesus marveled at her answer, and I marvel at her nerve. That's why she makes my list of *wonder* women.

Speak up or shut up

Every once in a while I need to lasso the Syrophoenician woman because I don't always handle my thoughts appropriately. At times, I have difficulty discerning when to express my thoughts and when to keep a lid on them. Do you?

You're in a board meeting, trying to be cooperative and a good team player, but something is put on the table that you don't agree with. Your heart starts pounding, and you'd like to speak up, but the other board members seem to be in agreement. No one else seems disturbed by the proposal.

You're in a committee meeting, one that you have been a part of on a regular basis for several years. You've noticed you don't really seem to be going anywhere because old methods keep being used. You're thinking that something new is needed. You hesitate to speak up because you like the women in the group; you don't want to ruffle any feathers or appear uncooperative.

You hear your pastor or a speaker teach something that is not quite right. It sounds good but isn't quite true. And then you wonder, *should I say anything? If so, when and how? Will I appear strident, bossy, pushy, or arrogant, or as a know-it-all, if I say something to the speaker?*

You read a blurb promoting a certain celebrity who is coming to a large church in your area. The blurb seems to downplay Jesus as the answer and promotes humor as *the* answer to the woes of women. Do you ignore it and let it go? Do you say something to the director of women's ministry? Do you contact the celebrity?

As we weigh these kinds of opportunities as to whether we will respond, this challenge is always before us: What kind of response would please Jesus?

We might ask ourselves questions like these:

- Can I express what I want to say in a way that will be respectful of the other person and of his or her position?
- Can I do it with lightness or wit as the Syrophoenician woman did and not threaten the others in the group?
- Do I have the right motive? Am I doing this out of love as the Syrophoenician woman acted out of love for her daughter? Do I have the best interests of others in mind?
- Will my response reflect my faith or encourage the faith of those I am questioning? Will it give Jesus a wider avenue for exercising grace?

If I can answer yes to these questions, then I lasso the Syrophoenician's courage, and speak up and trust that I will hear Jesus say to me as He did to her, "Way to go, Brenda! You are a woman of great faith!"

Becoming a *wonder* woman

How do you approach Jesus? Are you confident or timid?

When your plans are interrupted by someone outside of your geographical area, ethnic group or religious group, are you more likely to respond like the disciples or like Jesus?

How do the Syrophoenician woman's actions and words show faith?

What motivated her faith? Was her faith perfect? Is perfect faith necessary to having Jesus respond to us?

Just because you think something, should you say it? When should restraint be exercised?

Can a woman exercise control over what she says?

Chapter Fourteen

THE GALILEAN WOMEN

What Were You Thinking?

Matthew 27:55–56; Mark 15:40–41;
Luke 8:1–3, 23:49; 23:55 to 24:10; John 19:25–27

If you had a daughter who suddenly took up with a revolutionary, left home, and traveled with him and his cohorts, what would be your reaction?

Or what if a middle-aged friend decided to sell her business and support a rebel cause, what would you think?

Or what would you say if you had a friend who insisted on being present at the execution of a criminal? Would you try to talk her out of it?

If you would question the judgment of any one of these women, then you can imagine how people might have reacted to a group of Galilean women. This group of named[1] and unnamed women traveled with Jesus, supported His ministry, followed Him to the cross, and went to His tomb. At times people must have scratched their heads and wondered, *What are those women thinking?*

You traveled with whom?

Most Christians probably don't think of Jesus as a revolutionary. Because we know Jesus as loving, compassionate and kind, because we know that He did everything God wanted Him to do, it might not occur to us to think of Him as a rebel. But if we had been on the scene when He was here on earth, if we had seen how He butted heads with the religious leaders and challenged their rules, we might have thought otherwise.

Jesus deliberately broke the Sabbath laws and angered the scribes and Pharisees. He didn't break them just to break them; he broke those laws to get men and women to think and to show them a better way. He was on a mission to show what the Kingdom of God was really like. At first He did this in obscurity, but as He healed people and cast out demons, large crowds gathered to observe Him. As we learned in the last chapter, Herod Antipas, governor of Galilee, was fearful that Jesus would start an uprising, so he assigned people to keep an eye on Him.

Out of the people who followed Him, Jesus chose twelve men to accompany Him. Called apostles, they traveled with Him through towns and villages as He preached the good news about the Kingdom of God. On His second tour of Galilee, some women joined their entourage and traveled with them, and it was an outrageous thing to do. "The idea of a group of women going around with these men . . . was unheard of. Where did they sleep at night? Did they journey separately from the men? Why were they not at home looking after their own men folk? Women who traveled for other reasons than shopping and visiting relatives were always regarded with suspicion."[2] What were they thinking?

These women not only traveled with Jesus and the Twelve, they "used their own resources to help Jesus and his disciples" (Luke 8:3 GNT). What were their resources?

What did they have to give?

Their resources might have been financial. Luke 8:3 says they ministered to Jesus and the Twelve with "their substance" (KJV) or "their private means" (NASB). The Greek term Luke used was *ta hyparchonta*, literally "those (things) belonging to someone," in the sense of possessions. The same term is used in "sell your possessions, and give alms" (Luke 12:33 RSV), and "Truly, I say to you, he will set him over all his possessions" (Luke 12:44 RSV).

Whatever finances these women had would have been hard to come by. In much of the first century world, opportunities for women were limited. Generally, they could not own property or make tribal decisions. Their names were seldom listed in genealogical accounts. For the most part, men dominated in all power structures: civil, economic, military, and religious.

While women were restricted financially, it was possible that some of them had access to wealth or earned money in some way. Joanna, one of the named women, might have had some money because of her husband's position. As the steward of Herod Antipas, Chuza was the official who looked after the governor's financial interests and his private property. He may have been paid so well for his services that he agreed to let Joanna contribute to Jesus's ministry.

Since some of the women's names were listed without connection to a male name, the women might have been wealthy widows or they might have inherited property. Mosaic Law provided for a daughter to inherit her father's land if he had no sons (see Numbers 27:1–11).

It's also possible that the wealth of the Galilean women might have been from their own earnings. While the Bible does not give a specific example of a Galilean woman earning money, it does tell us that Lydia traded in purple cloth (Acts 16:11–15) and Priscilla, whose story we looked at in chapter 8, was a tentmaker. So this is a possibility.

Women who were independently wealthy were in the minority, not the majority. Most women weren't out in the marketplace, holding jobs and owning businesses. Consequently, friends and family members might have questioned the sanity of Galilean women using their hard-to-come-by money to support Jesus and the Twelve: "You mean you are in the enviable position of being wealthy, and you are going to spend money on a fringe group! Are you out of your mind? You're not going to get much return on your investment. Would-be messiahs come and go. Jesus is just one in a long line."

Instead of money, some scholars think these women offered housekeeping services for the men. The Bible says they "ministered unto him" (Luke 8:3 KJV). The Greek for the verb *ministered* means literally "who were serving them." It comes from the Greek verb *diakoneo*, meaning "to serve, to be an attendant, to wait upon menially as a servant, or to wait upon as a host, friend, or teacher."

The main idea behind *diakonos* is practical service, so the resources the Galilean women had to give may very well have been domestic abilities: cooking, cleaning, making beds, washing dishes, sweeping, or organizing. I'm sure some of their female friends questioned their going "on the road" to do the kinds of menial things they did at home only under rougher conditions. "You mean you are going to leave the comfort of home to build a campfire at a different place every night? Are you sure you want this camping experience? Have you thought this through?"

At least, though, they were doing these menial duties in Galilee. They weren't all that far from home, so their friends knew they could return home if they came to their senses. But when the Galilean women followed Jesus to Jerusalem, their female friends were really bewildered.

You're going where?

When the women first started traveling around Galilee, Jesus experienced high public favor, but opposition developed against Him. The Jewish religious leaders became upset with Him because He taught with authority and because He didn't observe many of their established observances and traditions. Consequently, the atmosphere around Jesus became tense. The opposition in Jerusalem in Judea, the center of Jewish orthodoxy, would be keen so it was risky for Jesus to leave Galilee to go there for the Passover. He went, anyway, and the Galilean women followed, including Jesus's mother.

Once in Jerusalem, it was hard to stay near Jesus. The city was crowded with people there for the Passover, and many of them wanted to be near Him. The Galilean women heard people speculate about Jesus's future. They heard religious leaders challenge and ridicule Him.

Then early on Friday morning they learned Jesus had been arrested by the Sanhedrin in the middle of the night.

They hung around the Roman headquarters hoping for Jesus's release, but when Pilate offered the crowd that possibility, they yelled, "Crucify him! Crucify him!"

The women winced at the sound as if a knife had been plunged into their hearts. This couldn't be happening! They looked around for the disciples but didn't see them anywhere.

They fell in with the crowd as it followed Jesus and the Roman soldiers to the crucifixion site. At the cross, they stood as close as they were allowed to go. Again they looked for the disciples, but could only find John. The spirit of the crowd was a malicious one, and hecklers shouted insults and taunts at the three to be crucified. Roman soldiers stood by keeping the crowd under control and seeing that no one interfered with the execution of Jesus and the two other men.

A crucifixion was a rough place to be and the sights and sounds were horrible. The Roman soldiers wondered, What are these women thinking to risk danger in order to be identified with Jesus? He's a criminal—do they want to be guilty by association? Who knows when the hostile crowds will start heckling them or when members of the Sanhedrin will accuse the women of wrongdoing as they have Jesus? A crowd like this is not to be trusted.

Crucifixion was one of the cruelest forms of punishment ever invented by man, so it is hard for us to understand why any woman would want to see such pain and suffering. Why would she put herself in a position to observe such hate, ridicule, and pain? Some of the bystanders looked at the women and thought. You look like good women. What are you doing at a place like this? Why don't you give up and go back home? There's nothing you can do here.

In a sense, the bystanders were right. The Galilean women had no power to free Jesus, no way to save him, no way to undo what had been done. Even if the Sanhedrin retried Jesus, the women would not be allowed to testify on Jesus's behalf because they did not regard the women as credible witnesses. Neither would the Galilean women have any influence with the mighty Roman Empire. There was nothing they could do to get the Roman procurator, Pontius Pilate, to reverse his decision.

Nevertheless, the women maintained their presence at the cross. Even when others questioned the wisdom of their being there, they stayed. As an awful darkness covered the earth, they did not leave. They were there right to the end, seeing His body taken down from the cross and watching to see where it was buried.

Joseph, a rich, pious Jew from Arimathea and a member of the Sanhedrin, saved the body of Jesus from the burning garbage heap, the usual place for crucifixion victims. Nicodemus, a Pharisee who once had a conversation with Jesus about being born again, helped him. The two of them partially prepared Jesus's body for burial, wrapped it in strips of linen and quickly placed it in a new tomb provided by Joseph. But they weren't able to finish the burial preparations because time was running out. The Sabbath, which began at sundown on Friday, was quickly approaching and all work must cease.

The women determined that they would return as soon as the Law permitted to finish ministrations to Jesus's body. These were emotionally and spiritually strong women, but were they physically strong? They would have to be if they were going to finish caring for Jesus's body, which would require getting the tomb open.

You think you are strong enough?

When the Galilean women followed Joseph and Nicodemus to the tomb, they took note of its location, its stone wheel door, and how Jesus's body was laid. They watched as the huge door was rolled into place and sealed by the Romans. They also noticed that Roman guards were assigned to watch the tomb.

On their way back to the places "where they were staying for the week, they secured materials for further anointing of the body. These they prepared in readiness for use at their first opportunity,"[3] which would be when the Sabbath ended. Early Sunday morning, just as the first beams of light were breaking through, they headed for the tomb, baskets of ointment and soft rags in hand. Shopkeepers getting ready for the day's business (the day after the Sabbath was a regular business day) noticed the women going by. They wondered, *What are those women doing out so early? It looks like they are going to the burial tombs. You've got to be kidding.*

I'm an early riser so I can understand their going early in the morning, and I can also understand their wanting to get there as soon as possible. But what I marvel at is their going with no idea how they would open the tomb.

"Tombs had no doors. When the word door is mentioned it really means opening. In front of the opening there ran a groove, and in the groove a circular stone as big as a cart-wheel."[4] The women knew that it was beyond their strength to move a stone like that, but they went, anyway. With their spices in hand, they walked toward the sepulcher and talked among themselves about how they might get the tomb opened (Mark 16:3).[5]

"Mary, how are we going to get into the tomb to anoint Jesus's body?"

"At this point, I'm not sure," Mary Magdalene replied as she continued to walk briskly.

"The door is so heavy and it was sealed by the Romans, remember?"

"Yes, I remember," she said as she continued to walk toward the tomb.

"And what about the guards?" asked Joanna. "Do you think the guards will let us near the tomb?"

"I can't answer all your questions, but you know what, I believe God will help us find a way. We must finish the burial preparations. We must do this for Jesus."

Anyone overhearing their conversation would have asked, "Are you women crazy? What makes you think you can roll that big stone away? Even if you could, the Roman soldiers guarding the tomb are not going to let you near it." But the women didn't listen to the voices on the sidelines; they didn't stop to consider what people might be thinking, and they weren't discouraged by impossibilities.

Family members, acquaintances, friends, soldiers, and even strangers must have wondered about Galilean women who exhibited such incredible behavior. What were they thinking?

To better understand these women—and to learn from them—I think it is important that we ask a second question: *What were they getting?*

They got to be with Jesus

Day in and day out, morning, noon, and evening on the second Galilean tour, these women got to be with Jesus. They had more time with Him than Martha and Mary did, who had occasional visits. As He preached to the multitudes, they were able to learn from Him. They were eyewitnesses to His miraculous power. Now wouldn't that be worth having friends and family question your sanity?

Helping Him by either giving money or doing menial chores, they got to express their gratitude. Many of the Galilean women who followed Jesus had been healed of evil spirits and diseases (Luke 8:3). They were so grateful that they wanted to give back so using their financial resources to support Jesus and the Twelve was a joy. While Jesus miraculously fed multitudes, he never used his divine power to provide for His own physical needs. During his three years of ministry, Jesus did not have a thing that He could call his own. He depended on the help of others, and the Galilean women counted it a privilege to be among those who helped.

They got to express their love. The women loved Jesus so much that they didn't think in terms of discomfort and they didn't count the cost of all the chores they did. When they were at the cross, they didn't think in terms of danger. They wanted to "be there" for Him. They knew their presence would minister to Jesus.

Being with Jesus, helping His ministry, they experienced purposeful living. Every day counted. They might have slept on the ground but when they got up each morning, they knew their life counted. They knew each completed chore was a contribution. It wasn't just washing dishes, it was washing dishes for Jesus! It wasn't just preparing supper, it was preparing refreshing nourishment for Jesus!

Jesus valued their contributions, respected them as persons, and affirmed their worth even when it might have discredited Him. His reputation was at stake, too, just as theirs was. Good Jewish men didn't associate with women in public. A Jewish rabbi might not even speak to his own wife or daughter or sister in public. If he did, it would be the end of his reputation! Curing women, associating with them, and choosing them to be among his followers all clearly dissociate Him from the times in which He lived. That was part of His rule-breaking! He talked openly with women, contrary to established custom and accepted teaching. He appreciated the services of the Galilean women and honored them by giving them a primary role in proclaiming His resurrection.

They got a sunrise surprise!

As it turned out, the women didn't have to roll away the stone at the tomb. When they arrived at the burial site, they saw that the great stone had been rolled away (Mark 16:4). They entered the tomb and found that Jesus's body was not there. Instead, an angel was. He gave them an urgent message—a message for them and the disciples. Jesus would meet them in Galilee (Matthew 28:5–8; Mark 16:5–7).

A little later, some of the women saw two men in dazzling apparel at the tomb and they offered the women words of comfort and instruction (Luke 24:4). The best part was the declaration, "He is not here, but is risen!" (Luke 24:5 NKJV).

They hurried to tell the disciples and other believers (Luke 24:8). As the significance of the empty tomb sank in, they returned to the tomb. As some of the women made their way towards it again, Mary Magdalene ran on ahead of them. She was alone when she saw the resurrected Jesus (John 20:11–18). Then Jesus appeared to the other women (Matthew 28:9–10). They fell down at his feet, held them and worshipped Him. The women had affirmed Jesus in His darkest hour, and now He affirmed them. He rewarded their faithfulness by appearing to them before anyone else saw Him.

When we faithfully follow Jesus, giving and ministering to Him no matter what others say—or think!, we will draw closer to Him and experience a purposeful existence. He will reveal Himself to us and teach us about Himself. We can know the fellowship of His sufferings and experience the power of the Resurrection (Philippians 3:10). We'll feel bubbling up inside us the realization that He is alive. We will experience the resurrected Jesus!

Becoming a *wonder* woman

What motivated the Galilean women to use their resources to help Jesus and the Twelve?

How were they rewarded for being present at the cross and for going to check on the body after the Sabbath was over?

In what ways did the Galilean women help Jesus?

Have you knowingly gone ahead and done something you knew other people questioned but you were certain God was leading you to do? What motivated you?

How much attention should we pay to what others think of what we do? When does it matter? And when does it not?

What kind of criticism have you received from those who are non-Christians about your behavior?

What kind of criticism have you received from those who are Christian sisters?

How did you respond?

Part V

SHE FELT HOW?

There is yet another type of biblical *wonder* woman: One who *experienced wonder*. We can experience *wonder* with regard to many things: ice shapes on a cold glass window, beautiful fall leaves, fireflies lighting up a woods, a child's innocence or energy! We can marvel at the nature of women. I hope as you have read so far you have experienced some rekindled *wonder* with regard to women, realizing anew what interesting, capable creatures we are.

Biblical women who experienced *wonder* were moved in their emotions and in their spirit by God. They were touched by God and responded in awe and humility. They experienced the *wonder* of God's awareness of them.

Chapter Fifteen

HAGAR

You Are the God Who Sees Me?

Genesis 16:1–16, 21:9–17, and 25:12

Hagar was a woman with limited choices. She was a slave, a handmaiden to Sarai, the wife of Abram, so she was told what to do. She had to leave her Egyptian home and dwell with them in Canaan, the land God earlier had promised to Abraham. Whatever Sarai wanted Hagar to do, she had to comply. Sarai's words were law.

Earlier Abram had received a promise from God that he would have many descendants, but as the years began to slip by, he and Hagar did not have even one child—let alone descendants. Eventually they grew tired of waiting for a child, and Sarai decided they should do something about it. Not even considering what Hagar might want or not want, Sarai gave her to Abram. She said, "You sleep with Hagar, and her children shall be mine," and that's how Hagar became pregnant through no choice of her own.

Two women, one husband

When Sarai gave her handmaiden to Abram, Hagar became a kind of second wife (called a concubine) to him. Clearly, this gesture was for sexual procreation because Sarai wanted children. Her action smacks of immorality and it is certainly immoral by today's standards, but what Sarai did was "a custom consistent with moral standards prevailing at that time."[1] In homes where there were no children, the children born to the union of a husband and a wife's servant were considered the children of the original wife.

Abram could have resisted Sarai's suggestion, but he didn't. He had a choice, but Hagar didn't. She had to submit her body to Abram, and consequently she soon became pregnant. Even though she was more bound than ever by her circumstances, she also began to see that she wasn't totally without options. She could choose how she responded to her mistress. One translation said Hagar "became very proud and arrogant toward her mistress Sarai" (Genesis 16:4 TLB). Another one said "she began to despise her mistress" (Genesis 16:4 NIV).

Her response could have been either or both. It could have been that she realized she was superior to her mistress in one sense. She could get pregnant and Sarai couldn't. She could carry a child in her womb and Sarai was barren. Or it could be that she despised her mistress for putting her in such a position, for not once considering what Hagar felt or wanted. She was in a predicament she didn't choose because Sarai called the shots.

Sarai noticed Hagar's attitude change and didn't like it. Interestingly, she responded not by raging at Hagar but by raging against her husband. She told Abram, "It's all your fault!" She said, "Now this servant girl of mine despises me, though I myself gave her the privilege of being your wife. May the Lord judge you for doing this to me!" (Genesis 16:5b TLB).

Perhaps she was struggling with guilt or regret over what she had done. Or perhaps what she seemed unable to do—have a child—became even clearer to her when Hagar's pregnancy began to show. She knew a child would result from their union—that was the goal—but she didn't realize the outcome would hurt so much.

Abram must have sensed her pain. Instead of reminding her that the idea had been hers, Abram said, "You can do anything you want to Hagar," so she did. She mistreated Hagar. One translation said she beat Hagar. It pains me to write that line. How much anger was involved in this beating? Was she like a parent punishing in anger instead of waiting to cool off first?

Whatever emotions were involved, compliant Hagar suddenly saw herself as having a choice—something she hadn't noticed before. She didn't have to tolerate Sarai's mistreatment; she could run away.

Desolate in the desert

That Hagar made a choice doesn't mean the choice was thought through. She fled without considering where she might live, how she might support herself, or what might happen to the baby in her womb.

She ran until she was exhausted. Out of breath and thirsty, she fell down near a well at a spring in the desert along the road to Shur. Hagar's pain was magnified by the reality of her circumstances. What in the world was she going to do?

At least, she was by a well; she would have water. She dared not venture out further into the desert, although she would have loved to return to Egypt to be with her people. She felt utterly alone as if no one was aware of her, but someone was. God was. God saw Hagar in her distress, and He sent an angel to minister to her.

The angel said, "Hagar, where have you come from and where are you going?"

Hagar answered, "I'm running away from my mistress." Notice that she answered the first part of the angel's question but not the second part. She stated exactly what she was doing: "I'm running away." She didn't amplify it with, "I've been with a mistress. I've been in the land of no choices. I've been mistreated."

But where was she going? That part of the question she did not—could not—answer. In her haste to get away, she hadn't thought ahead. It had been over ten years since she had left her Egyptian home to become Sarai's handmaiden. She was far away from family who might take her in. In her condition, it would never do for her to run further into the desert and try to live alone. She and her child might die.

God's angel, though, had a place for her to go. "The angel of the Lord told her, 'Go back to your mistress and submit to her'" (Genesis 16:9 NIV).

What? Go back! Go back to misery and being submissive? Go back to non-person status? That's my reaction, not Hagar's. I wish God would have miraculously provided for her in the wilderness so she didn't have to return to Sarai. That's the way I would have written the story, but God was doing the writing. His direction would seem cruel if He hadn't given Hagar something to take back with her.

What she returned with

Hagar needed to go back for the sake of her child—his future and hers. Their survival was at stake. Besides, God had plans for them. The angel said, "I will multiply thy seed exceedingly, that it shall not be numbered for multitude" (Genesis 16:10 KJV). That little baby growing inside her would have many descendants; God would develop a great nation from her offspring. This promise was a balm for Hagar's wounded spirit.

The angel went on to say, "Your baby will be a son, and you are to name him Ishmael ('God hears'), because God has heard your woes" (Genesis 16:11 TLB).

The angel described what her child would be like.

> He will be a wild donkey of a man;
> his hand will be against everyone
> and everyone's hand against him,
> and he will live in hostility
> toward all his brothers" (Genesis 16:12 NIV).

Not too many pregnant women would have been pleased with the angel's forecast, but his words were spirit-lifting to Hagar. Her son would be free and unrestrained! He would not have to live as she lived. He would not be a slave. He would have choices!

Hagar could not believe that she was getting this kind of attention from God. In awe she cried out, "Thou God seest me" (Genesis 16:13 KJV)—and that was what she took home with her. She wasn't forgotten, overlooked or utterly alone. This woman who had to respond to authority—this woman who had felt like a non-person—realized she wasn't. God saw her! In amazement, she "asked herself, 'Have I really seen God and lived to tell about it?'" (Genesis 16:13 GNT). In her way, she was saying, "This is just too good to be true!" And she definitely lived to tell about it! As Hagar shared her story, others rejoiced with her and called the well where God's angel appeared to her "The Well of the Living One Who Sees Me" (Genesis 16:14 GNT).

As she went about her daily duties back at Sarai's house, as she complied with her wishes, she sang over and over, "Thou God seest me." She didn't sing the words loudly or arrogantly, it was a song she sang to herself. It was a song of the heart—one that she could hear and be comforted by. The song put a spring in her step and gave her the grace to handle her circumstances.

Wonder does that. *Wonder* is a spiritual and emotional experience to be treasured in and of itself, but it also helps us live with circumstances we cannot change. Much of the time we can change our circumstances, but sometimes we can't. Sometimes we come up against hard, unchangeable circumstances, and it helps immensely to know in a glorious way that God is aware of us. It helps us live with what we cannot change.

It was no easy matter for Hagar to return and to submit to Sarai, but it was the right thing to do, and the *wonder* of God seeing her, God's awareness of her, enabled her to go back *and to stay*. Her circumstances had not changed but she had. If anything, they became more complicated as she gave birth to Ishmael, adding the presence of a child to the triangle of tension.

When three became four and then five

After Hagar returned to live with Sarai and Abram, she gave birth to a son. Abram was 86 years of age at the time.

Abram named Hagar's boy Ishmael, which means that he must have listened to and accepted Hagar's story about God's angel appearing to her. He believed that Ishmael would be the leader of a great nation, and for a time, he may have thought God's promise to him was going to be fulfilled through Ishmael. Her story may have also changed Abram's attitude about her. Forced sexual relations apparently stopped because no more children were born to Abram and Hagar.

This doesn't mean, though, that all the tension was eliminated from the household. Everyday the presence of Ishmael was a reminder to Sarai that she was barren. While she was the real wife, she was not the real mother. The Bible never indicates in any way that Sarai got to become the mother of Ishmael as she had anticipated when she gave Hagar to Abram.

As one year after another passed with no more children being born, Abram became quite fond of little Ishmael. When God told him that he was still going to have a child with Sarai—yes, Sarai was finally going to get to be a mother—Abram implored God, "Why not let Ishmael be my heir?" (17:18 GNT).

God assured Abram that Ishmael would become the ancestor of a great nation, just as he promised Hagar, but His covenant that He had made years earlier with Abram would be carried out through the child he and Sarai would have. At this time, Abram was 99 years old.

God confirmed his covenant promise to Abram by changing his name from Abram (meaning "exalted father") to Abraham ("father of many") and changing Sarai's name to Sarah. When the long-awaited heir arrived, Abraham had reached his 100th birthday, and Sarah was 90. The baby was a boy, and the parents named him Isaac. God's promise to Abraham was materializing, and Sarah was finally a mother. I wish we could say that the five lived happily ever after, but we can't. Sarah's discomfort with Hagar still existed, and it surfaced as she watched the children interact.

Boys will be boys

When Isaac was old enough to be weaned, Abraham gave a party to celebrate the happy occasion. Ishmael and little Isaac interacted at the party, and Sarah didn't like it. Exactly what the nature of their interaction was, the Bible doesn't say. *The Living Bible* does say Ishmael was teasing little Isaac (Genesis 21:9), and he may have said, "Mom, make him quit." Maybe they were wrestling together and Sarah was afraid Isaac would get hurt. Maybe the bigger boy was tousling little Isaac's hair, and Abraham laughed as he watched the love between them, and Sarah couldn't stand that Ishmael was also Abraham's son, his firstborn, no less. She turned to Abraham, and in that strong way of hers she demanded, "Get rid of that slave girl and her son. He is not going to share your property with my son. *I won't have it*" (Genesis 21:10 TLB; author's italics). Her words were cruel—she did not even call Hagar and Ishmael by their names. They were "that slave girl and her son."

Sarah's actions "upset Abraham very much, for after all, Ishmael too was his son" (Genesis 21:11 TLB).

"But God told Abraham, 'Don't be upset over the boy or your slave-girl wife; do as Sarah says, for Isaac is the son through whom my promise will be fulfilled. And I will make a nation of the descendants of the slave girl's son, too, because he also is yours" (Genesis 21:12–13 TLB).

"So Abraham got up early the next morning, prepared food for the journey, and strapped a canteen of water to Hagar's shoulders and sent her away with their son" (Genesis 21:14 TLB). It was not her choice, but she and Ishmael had to go. Whatever were they going to do?

When heaven heard their weeping

Hagar and Ishmael walked out into the wilderness of Beersheba. Fourteen years had passed since she ran away, and here she was aimless again. Beersheba lay on the edge of a vast wilderness that stretched as far as Egypt to the southwest and Mount Sinai to the south. Several wells were in the area. Perhaps if they could just make it to one of the wells, Hagar could think and figure out what to do, but none was in sight.

She was just so unprepared for this forced change in her life. Once she had gone back and had been submissive to Sarai as God had told her to, she had never dreamed that she would be sent away, but here she was, wandering and *wonder*ing in the desert. Where can we go? How am I going to take care of my son? What are we going to do?

In the hot desert, they soon drank all the water in their canteen and that added another, larger worry. Are we going to die from hunger and thirst in this barren land? If I could just find one of the wells in this area, I can get my bearings.

Ishmael already was becoming weak from dehydration. Was he going to die? She couldn't bear the thought. She helped him lie down under a bush out of the heat and then she went about a hundred yards away and sat down. This way, she could keep an eye on him while trying to figure out what to do. The thought of his dying was almost more than she could bear, and she began crying. Her tears joined those of Ishmael, who was already crying.

God heard their crying and responded. "From heaven the angel of God spoke to Hagar, 'What are you troubled about, Hagar?'" (Genesis 21:17 GNT).

The last time God's angel had appeared to Hagar, he had asked her a question. He was asking again, "What are you troubled about, Hagar?" The angel was God's messenger, and God had seen Hagar. He knew what was happening, so why the questions?

A question can quell emotions, and Hagar was very emotional. A question makes a person stop and think, breaking up hardened thought patterns, leading to a broader look or seeing other options. Thinking heightens alertness. An alert mind is more likely to experience *wonder* than a passive mind. The right kind of question softens the soul, improving our receptivity to hear from God and recognize Him. We can't just click on a "*wonder* button" and have a "*wonder* experience" suddenly appear on the screen of life. We must nurture our spiritual receptivity and the right questions can help us do that.

Certain that she was ready to receive, God's angel continued. He said, "Don't be afraid, Hagar. God has heard the boy crying. Get up, go, hold him, and comfort him. I will make a great nation out of his descendants" (Genesis 21:17-18 GNT).

And then the supernatural happened—God opened her eyes. She could see. She saw a well. She went and filled the leather bag with water and gave some to Ishmael. As he held the bag to his lips, she felt renewed strength. God was aware of her; He had promised that her child would be the head of a great nation. He would not abandon them. He would provide. The God who sees is the God who hears.

As the color returned to Ishmael's face, she felt strength and resolve return to her body. As she experienced the *wonder* of the God who hears, she went from hopeless to hopeful, from "I can't" to "I can." Within her innermost being—where it counts—she knew she could be a mother in the desert. She was more mature than she had been fourteen years earlier, and she wasn't pregnant. She could help her son grow into a man and even find a wife for him, which she did.

Ishmael's name, meaning "God hears," was now fully appreciated by Hagar. In the wilderness, God heard the moaning of a mother's heart and a boy's cry. From then on, every time she called Ishmael's name, every time she heard his name mentioned, she was reminded that God hears. Her song, "Thou God seest me," continued to resonate within her, but now there was a second verse: "Thou God hearest me."

Becoming a *wonder* woman

What questions did God's angel ask Hagar?

Were those questions related in any way to Hagar's experiencing *wonder*?

What might experiencing *wonder* do for our lives?

What connections might tears have with experiencing *wonder*?

Where have you seen God lately? As a result of that encounter, what name would you give to the place where you saw Him?

How was the outcome of Hagar's second *wonder* experience different from the first? Why do you think there was a difference?

Chapter Sixteen

ELIZABETH

Who Am I That This Should Happen to Me?

Luke 1:5–80

Many hundreds of years after Sarah miraculously became pregnant and gave birth to Isaac, another old woman—the Bible's words, not mine!—became pregnant. Her name was Elizabeth and she lived when Herod was the Roman appointed head of Palestine. At this time, the Jews longed for a Messiah—an anointed Deliverer that would set them free from Roman rule and put them in charge. Because there was so much talk about this, Elizabeth often found herself thinking about the Deliverer as she went about her household duties. She was more apt to do this when her priest-husband, Zechariah, went to do his yearly duties at the temple in Jerusalem. As she reflected, she had no idea that she might have a part in the drama that would usher in the Messiah's appearance.

The desire for a child

Like Sarah, Elizabeth was barren. Unlike Sarah, she did not mistreat anyone or manipulate circumstances to try to get a child. Elizabeth and her husband Zechariah "were both righteous before God" (Luke 1:6 KJV). They "lived good lives in God's sight and obeyed fully all the Lord's laws and commands" (Luke 1:6 GNT).

Even though Elizabeth lived centuries after Sarah, they both lived in cultures that considered having children important. Children brought joy to a home. Children provided security for adults in their later years. Children were a sign of God's favor. Children carried on your name, passed on your faith and rituals, and inherited your property. A woman's worth and hope were measured by her children; Elizabeth had none. Zechariah could have divorced her for this, but he didn't. He loved Elizabeth, and together they focused on doing God's will.

In the early years of their marriage, they assumed a child would quickly bless their home. When a little one didn't arrive, they prayed for a child. In their twenties and thirties, and even on into middle age, they kept thinking "any day now" Elizabeth would get pregnant, but she didn't. At times, the disappointment was almost more than they could bear, and they couldn't have borne it if they hadn't held on in faith. They never really gave up hope, and yet, it was still a shock—at least it was for Zechariah—when they found out they were going to have a baby.

A baby? You mean us?

Zechariah learned they were going to have a baby when he was doing his priestly duties in the temple. The angel

Gabriel appeared to him, and Zechariah "was alarmed and felt afraid" (Luke 1:12*a* GNT).

Gabriel quickly reassured him, "Don't be afraid, Zechariah! God has heard your prayer, and your wife Elizabeth will bear you a son" (Luke 1:13*a* GNT).

Gabriel went on to say, "He will be a great man in the Lord's sight. He must not drink any wine or strong drink. From his very birth he will be filled with the Holy Spirit, and he will bring back many of the people of Israel to the Lord their God. He will go ahead of the Lord, strong and mighty like the prophet Elijah. He will bring fathers and children together again; he will turn disobedient people back to the way of thinking of the righteous; he will get the Lord's people ready for Him" (Luke 1:14–17 GNT).

This announcement was too much for Zechariah. The angel's words didn't jibe with reality. "Zechariah said to the angel, 'How shall I know if this is so? I am an old man, and my wife is old also" (Luke 1:18 GNT).

Gabriel replied, "I stand in the presence of God, who sent me to speak to you and tell you this good news. But you have not believed my message, which will come true at the right time. Because you have not believed, you will be unable to speak; you will remain silent until the day my promise to you comes true" (Luke 1:19–20 GNT).

How frustrating this must have been for Zechariah to have such great news and not be able to verbalize it when he got home! Elizabeth was alarmed by his inability to speak. What had happened to Zechariah while he was away? Why couldn't he talk? She could tell he wanted—no, needed—to talk. She got him a wax writing tablet and a stylus, and he wrote quickly, "We're going to have a baby!"

With a raised eyebrow, she looked at him and said affectionately, "What happened to you, old man, while you were in Jerusalem?"

He pointed to the tablet again as if to emphasize the truth, "We're going to have a baby!"

She looked toward him with a doubtful look on her face. He looked back at her, shook his head up and down, indicating they were indeed going to have a baby.

Her heart started racing. A child at last? My very own child to hold in my arms? A child to bring us joy and pleasure in our old age? And challenges, too! Many different kinds of feelings began competing for attention as she took in Zechariah's news.

Zechariah touched her on the arm and motioned for her to look at the tablet as he scraped off the words and began writing again. She was intrigued. Was there more to the story? But what else could there be? Wasn't just knowing they were going to have a baby enough?

The rest of the story

It was a laborious, tedious task for Zechariah as he tried to write down all that happened in the temple. In her excitement, Elizabeth could hardly concentrate, and yet she could tell every word was important to Zechariah. If he could just talk . . . Elizabeth still didn't understand what happened to his speech.

Elizabeth tried to focus on the words on the wax tablet before they had to be scraped off for a new set. Little by little, it became clear to her that an angel had visited Zechariah while he performed his temple duties. That's how he knew they would have a child—indeed, a son. It was because

Gabriel had told him. Gabriel had said their son would be special, strong and mighty like the prophet Elijah. Their child's appearing would precede the coming of the Messiah, the longed-for, expected Deliverer. This child would be special—he would be the preparer of the Way, making the road ready for the coming of the Messiah. He would go before the Messiah, getting the people ready for Him.

Elizabeth studied Zechariah's words, trying to comprehend what they said and what they meant. The concepts were almost mind-boggling, but Elizabeth believed Zechariah and she believed God. Her heart beat with the certainty that at last, after all those years of praying, God was going to fulfill her heart's desire. But what about the prophecy that her son would be a forerunner for the Messiah? Was the Messiah really going to come?

Time to think

Elizabeth responded to Zechariah's news and her subsequent pregnancy by going into seclusion. You might think it odd that a woman who always wanted to be pregnant didn't rush out and tell her neighbors the news. But think again. What would people's reactions be? She was past child-bearing age. If she told, others would speculate and talk about her. Did she really want her joy to be dampened by people's reactions? Staying home alone, she could keep the good news to herself, hold it close and rejoice in it.

Mixed in with her joy was concern about their future. She and Zechariah would be having a baby while their friends were having grandchildren and some of their friends were even past that stage already. They would be out of sync. She thought a lot about how their lives were going to change, how they could relate to their son, and even if they would live long enough to see him to adulthood.

And what about those prophecies about their son's future? Gabriel said he would be like Elijah. Did that mean he would be odd? Elijah certainly had had his odd moments. Gabriel had said their son would be the preparer of the Way for the Messiah. Did that mean the Messiah was coming soon? Would he be born in the near future? Would he be a contemporary of their son? And then a new thought occurred to her . . . kind of an "aha" thought . . . one that Zechariah hadn't even hinted at. If the Messiah were going to be born soon, then somewhere another woman was pregnant or was going to be pregnant. Somewhere was the Messiah's mother. Who would that woman be?

A meeting of mothers

What Elizabeth didn't know was that the angel who had appeared to her husband in the temple in Jerusalem would also appear to her young cousin in another part of Palestine. Six months after Gabriel appeared to Zechariah, he appeared to Mary in Nazareth of Galilee.

Gabriel said to Mary, "Rejoice, highly favored one, the Lord is with you; blessed are you among women!" (Luke 1:28 NKJV).

Gabriel assured her that she had found favor with God. God was blessing her. Gabriel then made a startling announcement: "You will become pregnant and give birth to a son, and you will name him Jesus. He will be great and will be called the Son of the Most High God" (Luke 1:31–32 GNT).

Mary did not doubt, but she was genuinely puzzled. She said, "I am a virgin. How, then, can this be?"

Gabriel explained that the conception would be an act of the Holy Spirit. The creative power of God would overshadow her and make this possible.

Still, the idea of becoming pregnant without knowing a man seemed impossible to Mary. Gabriel assured her by telling her about another supernatural happening. He said, "Remember your relative Elizabeth. It is said that she cannot have children, but she herself is now six months pregnant, even though she is very old. For there is nothing that God cannot do" (Luke 1:36–37 GNT).

Mary hastened off to the hill country in Judea where Elizabeth lived. She had to talk to someone who would understand this unusual happening in her life.

Mary knew about Elizabeth's condition because Gabriel had told her, but Elizabeth didn't know about Mary's situation. She didn't know that Mary had a visit from the same angel who had spoken to Zechariah. She didn't know that Mary was pregnant when she opened the door. The trip from Nazareth to Elizabeth's house in Judea took only a few days so Mary's pregnancy wasn't visible yet.

When Elizabeth heard Mary's greeting, her baby moved within her. The movement coincided with Mary's greeting, as if the baby recognized Mary's voice. It was not a flutter; the baby "leaped in her womb" (Luke 1:41 NKJV). Occurring forcefully when it did, the movement reminded Elizabeth of Gabriel's words to her husband about their baby: "He will be filled with the Holy Spirit while yet in his mother's womb" (Luke 1:15 NASB). The joy of this realization prompted a swelling of the Holy Spirit within Elizabeth and she put together what no one had spelled out for her. This woman knocking at her door was the mother of God's Anointed, the mother of the promised Messiah! Elizabeth realized Mary was the mother of the One for whom her son was to prepare the way. In a loud voice, she said to Mary, "You are the most blessed of all women, and blessed is the child you will bear!" (Luke 1:42*b* GNT).

Ecstatic with wonder, Elizabeth said, "Why should this great thing happen to me, that my Lord's mother comes to visit me?" (Luke 1:43 GNT). She was filled with awe and humility.

Zechariah had had his supernatural moment when Gabriel visited him in the temple. Mary had had hers when Gabriel visited her in Nazareth. And now Elizabeth had hers, and she was humbled by it. Why should this great thing happen to me? You mean me? You mean God sees me? Do you mean I have a part in this great drama?

There was childlike amazement and joy in Elizabeth's response. It could have been any number of other women, but God chose her, and she was amazed. Elizabeth's response is in stark contrast to Sarah's when she had an opportunity to marvel at God. When God was involving her in a great drama, she was skeptical.

Two women, two views

After Ishmael was born but before Isaac was born, three angels appeared at Abraham and Sarah's camp (Genesis 18:1–15). At this time, Sarah was nearly 90 years old and Abraham was near 100. Sarah didn't talk directly to the angels. She was standing behind Abraham, taking it all in and listening to Abraham's conversation with them. They said, "Where is your wife?"

Abraham said, "She is in the tent."

One angel said, "I'll be back in the spring, and by that time Sarah will have a son." Sarah laughed, but her laughter was not the laughter of joy that sometimes occurs with an experience of wonder. It was the laughter of a person whose sense of wonder had died long ago.

We are all born with a sense of wonder, but it can get eroded by life experiences, and Sarah certainly had more than her fair share: several geographical moves (none of her choosing), leaving her extended family behind, disappointment over not having a baby, being lied about by her husband, taken away from her husband for a time by an Egyptian king, and the ongoing tension with Hagar. So these experiences could explain the difference; while Elizabeth's life knew the disappointment of not having children, it had still been a good stable life with a solid marriage to Zechariah.

Our sense of wonder can also be undermined by rationality. Because the hard facts of biology were staring Sarah in the face, she was not awed by God's announcement. She and Abraham were just too old to have a baby. The hard facts may also have been why Zechariah hadn't responded to Gabriel with wonder. When told he and Elizabeth were going to have a child, he said, "I am an old man, and my wife is old also" (Luke 1:18 GNT). This is not to suggest that we shouldn't pursue facts; that statement would undermine what I said about wisdom and knowledge in chapter 12. But in gaining knowledge, we should keep in mind that we worship a God of the impossible.

Our sense of wonder can also be affected by sin in our lives. We all make mistakes. Some of those mistakes are like the ones Sarah made: mistreating others, manipulating people, and being jealous and angry. If we do not confess those sins and seek God's forgiveness, a dark residue settles in our inner space—the place where our sense of wonder dwells. The more sin in our lives, the less room there is for wonder.

Sarah was still sinning as the angels, God's messengers, were conversing with Abraham. They heard her laugh and when the Lord (through an angel) wanted to know why, Sarah protested and said, "I didn't laugh," but she did. She lied—further evidence of the life she was living—the kind of life that stifles wonder.

In contrast, Elizabeth "obeyed fully all the Lord's laws and commands" (Luke 1:6 GNT). She was one of a few people described in the Bible as living a "good" life (GNT) or a life "upright in the sight of God" (NIV). The faith of people who live this kind of life often takes on a childlike quality, so pure is their trust in God. Their sense of wonder is intact. Sometimes their faith seems too simple for me with my analytical mind. They often appear naïve. And yet I like to be around them for they kindle my own sense of wonder, something I want to hold on to. Do you?

Which view for you?

Which woman do you want to be? Do you want to be cynical like Sarah, dead to wonder? Or do you want to be amazed like Elizabeth, alive to wonder?

It's not a choice you *have* to make. Wonder is not necessary to the Christian life. It has nothing to do with whether you will go to heaven. It is not necessary for solving many of life's problems. Neither is it necessary to having God work in your life. Sarah's lack of wonder did not thwart

God's promise to Abraham; an heir, Isaac, was born to them. Zechariah's rational response resulted in a temporary loss of speech, but he and Elizabeth still gave birth to the preparer of the Way for the Messiah. Wonder is not necessary for being used by God, but it is something that greatly enriches the Christian life.

I want that enrichment. I want those moments when I can exuberantly say, "Why has this great thing happened to me?" And that's why I study women of the Bible so I can be reminded of what God can do and wants to do with women. That's why I need Elizabeth as one of my *wonder* women. She reminds me that being good is important to keeping my sense of wonder alive.

You may protest and say, "I could never be as good as Elizabeth." I understand; I can't either. That's why I have to continually be confessing sin, mending fences, letting go of hurts and acknowledging trust in Jesus Christ so there will be room in my inner space for wonder to reside and thrive. Dealing with sin is not the only thing I do, but it is one of the most important things that I do—because if I don't, my sin will work against all of my other efforts.

We can't determine when we will experience wonder. We can't program God to respond at a certain time or at a certain place, but we can be ready so that when the heavens open and His love shines through, we can feel the glow and respond as Hagar did, "Thou God seest me." Or when He arranges a supernatural experience as He did when Mary visited Elizabeth, we can exclaim as she did, "You mean me? You mean you love me this much? Who am I to have this great thing happen to me?" Now that's the kind of *wonder* woman that I most want to be.

Becoming a *wonder* woman

The three strangers (angels) who visited Abraham and Sarah and the angel Gabriel, who visited Zechariah and Mary, were God's messengers. Who visits you? Would you recognize them as God's messengers?

Who can experience wonder?

What is the experience like?

What is your response to the question, "Is anything too hard for God?" What does your response say about your sense of wonder?

What erodes a woman's sense of wonder?

How does a sense of wonder relate to the Christian life?

CONCLUSION

Who Are Your *Wonder* Women?

To look at the Bible's *wonder* women is not to imply that there is some kind of "ideal *wonder* woman" we all should aspire to be. If that were the case, all of the women featured in this book would have been very much alike, and they weren't.

As you can tell from reading this book, the Bible's *wonder* women were very different from each other, living at different times and in varied situations. Some had exemplary character but others were engaged in doing things that Christian women should not imitate. This is encouraging because it means in our proneness toward sin, we can still be used by God. What was possible in their lives is possible in ours. Their stories are hope builders, and I learned from all of them.

I hope as I described some of their attributes and explored their lives, that those descriptions were insightful to you. I hope they raised your consciousness about the *wonder* of being a woman and the God we serve.

The Bible's *wonder* women weren't perfect, but they

were real. One reason I didn't read *Wonder* Woman comics when I was a child was because I was a realist even then. If something supernatural occurred, I wanted to know it was God's doing and not fantasy. When everything works out, I want to know if it was real. If it was, then the same possibilities exist for me.

What about you? Who is on your list? Who are the *wonder* women in your life? Who are the women who inspire you?

Some of the women on my list may be on your list, but our lists won't be exactly the same, and they shouldn't be. Each of our lists should be women who inspire us depending on our individual natures, our circumstances and our spiritual maturity.

Take some time to think about who is on your list and write their names here:

Whose example makes you stronger? Who reminds you that women are capable, interesting people? Whose incredible acts light up your life? What women remind you that you can experience wonder? Who gives you a glimpse of how you want to be?

The women on your *wonder* women list may be women from the Bible as mine are. They could be historical women or they could be women you know—women in your family, in your church, at your work, in your activities, or among your friends. Write their names here:

Doing so will help you stop and think about who they are. As you do, you will find as I did that you assess your self, raise your appreciation level of women, and strengthen your relationship with God.

You may want simply to record each name. Or you may want to write each woman's contribution to your life by her name. What is it about her that inspires you?

If you have a number of names you may want to divide them in categories as I did:

- Strong Women: Rahab, Deborah, Esther
- Wonderful Women: Ruth and Dorcas
- Women Who Work Wonders: Anna, Martha, Priscilla, Phoebe
- Women Who Do Incredible Things: Jael, Abigail, Wise Woman of Abel, the Syrophoenician woman, and the Galilean women
- Women Who Experience Wonder: Hagar and Elizabeth

If your *wonder* women list comes from women you know, you might want to follow through by writing them a note, thanking them and letting them know what you admire about them. If they are biblical women or historical women, say a prayer and thank God for them. Wherever they are from, lasso their examples in your life. No better tribute could be paid.

ENDNOTES

Chapter 1

[1]Rabbi Joseph Telushkin, *Biblical Literacy: The Most Important People, Events and Ideas of the Hebrew Bible* (New York: William Morrow and Company, Inc., 1997), 158.

[2]Herbert Lockyer, *All the Women of the Bible* (Grand Rapids: Zondervan Publishing House, 1988), 132.

[3]William Barclay, *The Letter to Hebrews The Daily Study Bible* (Edinburgh, Scotland: Saint Andrew Press, 1955, 1957), 183–84.

Chapter 2

[1]Elizabeth Deen, *All the Women of the Bible* (New York: Harper & Row, 1955), 72.

Chapter 6

[1]Carol Meyers, gen. ed, Toni Craven and Ross S. Kraemer, assoc. eds., *Women in Scripture* (New York: Houghton Mifflin Co., 2000), 51.

[2]Herbert Lockyer, *All the Women of the Bible* (Grand Rapids: Zondervan Publishing House, 1988), 30.

[3]William Barclay, *The Gospel of Luke*, *The Daily Study Bible* (Edinburgh, Scotland: Saint Andrew Press, 1964), 19.

[4]Lockyer, *All the Women of the Bible*, 31.

Chapter 7

[1]W. Hunt Gloer, *As You Go . . . An Honest Look at the First Followers of Jesus* (Macon, GA: Peake Road, 1996), 98.

Chapter 8

[1]William Barclay, *The Letter to the Romans, The Daily Study Bible* (Edinburgh, Scotland: Saint Andrew Press, 1955, 1957), 228.

[2]Ibid., 229.

[3]Jo Berry, *The Priscilla Principle: Making Your Life a Ministry*. (Grand Rapids: Zondervan Publishing House, 1984), 54.

Chapter 9

[1]*The Interpreter's Dictionary of the Bible*, R-Z (Nashville: Abingdon Press, 1962), 692.

[2]14 Jerome Murphy-O'Conner, O.P., "On the Road and on the Sea with St. Paul: Traveling Conditions in the First Century" (http://www.bib-arch.org/On_the_Road.pdf.), 3.

[3]Ibid., 8.

[4]Ibid.

Chapter 10

[1]From "The Spider and the Fly," a poem by Mary Howitt (1799–1888), published in 1829 in The New Year's Gift and Juvenile.

[2]Ibid.

[3]Melvin Konner, *The Tangled Wing* (New York: Holt, Rinehart and Winston, 1982), 109.

[4]Tim Molloy, "Police Find Possible 7th Shooting Victim," Associated Press, February 1, 2006.

[5]Brenda Poinsett, *I'm Glad I'm a Woman* (Wheaton, IL: Tyndale House Publishers, Inc., 1988), 35.

[6]Gleason Archer, *Encyclopedia of Bible Difficulties* (Grand Rapids: Zondervan Publishing House, 1982), 163.

Chapter 12

[1]Joe O. Lewis, *Layman's Bible Book Commentary:1 & 2 Samuel, 1 Chronicles*, Volume 5 (Nashville: Broadman Press, 1980), 115.

[2]*The Interpreter's Bible*, Volume 2 (Nashville: Abingdon Press, 1953), 1154.

[3]Ibid.

Chapter 13

[1]My interpretation that this is spoken to the disciples is based on the commentary in *Hard Sayings of Jesus's* by F. F. Bruce (Downers Grove, IL: InterVarsity Press, 1983), 110–11.

[2]John Trigilio Jr., PhD, ThD, and Kenneth Brighenti, PhD, *Women in the Bible for Dummies* (Hoboken, NJ: Wiley Publishing, Inc., 2005), 185.

[3]Dwight Moody, T. De Witt Talmage, and Joseph Parker, *Bible Characters* (Chicago: Thos. W. Jackson Publishing Company, 1902), 265.

[4]*The Interpreter's Bible*, Volume 7 (Nashville: Abingdon Press, 1951), 441.

Chapter 14

[1]The named women were Mary Magdalene, Joanna, Susanna, Mary (the mother of James the Less and Joses), Mary (the wife of Clopas) Salome, and Mary (the mother of Jesus). The names don't always appear all together although Mary Magdalene seems to appear in every named grouping.

[2]Ross Saunders, *Outrageous Women, Outrageous God* (Alexandria, Australia: E. J. Dwyer, 1996), 61–62.

[3]Ray Summers, *Commentary on Luke* (Waco, TX: Word Books, 1972), 315.

[4]William Barclay, *The Gospel of Mark*, 3d ed., *The Daily Study Bible* (Edinburgh, Scotland: Saint Andrew Press, 1956, 1964), 387.

[5]The sequencing of the women going to the tomb, their seeing the angels and their seeing the resurrected Jesus was garnered from *A Harmony of the Gospels for Students of the Life of Christ* by A. T. Robertson. New York: Harper and Brothers Publishers. 1950.

Chapter 15

[1]Herbert Lockyer, *All the Women of the Bible* (Grand Rapid: Zondervan Publishing House, 1988), 62.

BIBLIOGRAPHY

Archer, Gleason. *Encyclopedia of Bible Difficulties*. Grand Rapids: Zondervan Publishing House, 1982.

Barclay, William. *The Letter to Hebrews, The Daily Study Bible*. Edinburgh, Scotland: Saint Andrew Press, 1955, 1957.

________. *The Letter to the Romans, The Daily Study Bible*. Edinburgh, Scotland: Saint Andrew Press, 1955, 1957.

Berry, Jo. *The Priscilla Principle: Making Your Life a Ministry*. Grand Rapids: Zondervan, 1984.

Bruce, F. F. *Hard Sayings of Jesus*. Downers Grove, IL: InterVarsity Press, 1983.

Deen, Edith. *All the Women of the Bible*. New York: Harper and Row Publishers—Harper Collins Publishers Inc., 1955.

Hester, H. I. *The Heart of the New Testament*. Liberty, MO: William Jewell Press, 1950.

________. *The Heart of Hebrew History*. Liberty, Mo: William Jewell Press, 1949.

House, Paul R. *Old Testament Survey*. Nashville: Broadman Press, 1992.

Life Application Bible. Wheaton, IL: Tyndale House Publishers, 1988.

Lewis, Joe O. *Layman's Bible Book Commentary: 1 & 2 Samuel, 1 Chronicles*, Volume 5. Nashville: Broadman Press, 1980.

Lockyer, Herbert. *All the Women of the Bible*. Grand Rapids: Zondervan Publishing House, 1988.

Moody, Dwight, T. De Witt Talmage, and Joseph Parker. *Bible Characters*. Chicago: Thos. W. Jackson Publishing Company, 1902.

Murphy-O'Conner, O. P., Jerome. "On the Road and on the Sea with St. Paul: Traveling Conditions in the First Century," http://www.bib-arch.org/On_the_Road.pdf.

Myers, Carol, general editor with Toni Craven and Ross S. Kraemer, associate editors. *Women in Scripture*. New York: Houghton Mifflin Co., 2000.

Owens, Virginia Stem. *Daughters of Eve*. Colorado Springs, CO: NavPress, 1995.

Patterson, Dorothy Kelley, and Rhonda Harrington Kelley, eds. *The Woman's Study Bible: Opening the Word of God to Women*. Nashville: Thomas Nelson Publishers, 1995.

Poinsett, Brenda. *She Walked with Jesus*. Birmingham, AL: New Hope Publishers, 2004.

________. *When Saints Sing the Blues*. Grand Rapids: Baker Publishing Group, 2006.

Radius, Marianne. Two Spies on a Rooftop. Grand Rapids: Baker Book House, 1968. Formerly published under the title The Tent of God. William B. Eerdmans Publishing Company, 1968.

Saunders, Ross. *Outrageous Women, Outrageous God.* Alexandria, Australia: E. J. Dwyer, 1996.

Schultz, Samuel J., and Gary V. Smith. *Exploring the Old Testament.* Wheaton, IL: Crossway Books, 2001.

Summers, Ray. *Commentary on Luke.* Waco, TX: Word Books, 1972.

Telushkin, Rabbi Joseph. *Biblical Literacy: The Most Important People, Events and Ideas of the Hebrew Bible.* New York: William Morrow and Company, Inc., 1997.

The Interpreter's Bible. Volumes 2, 7. Nashville: Abingdon, 1953. Editors: Buttrick, George Arthur, Commentary editor, with Walter Russell Bowie, Associate Editor of Exposition, Paul Scherer, Associate Editor of Exposition, John Knox, Associate Editor of New Testament Introduction and Exegesis, Samuel Terrien, Associate Editor of Old Testament Introduction and Exegesis, and Nolan B. Harmon, Editor, Abingdon Press]

The Interpreter's Dictionary of the Bible, R-Z. Nashville: Abingdon, 1962. Buttrick, George Arthur, Dictionary Editor, with Thomas Samuel Kepler, Associate Editor of New Testament Articles, Illustrations, John Knox, Associate Editor of New Testament Articles, Herbert Gordon May, Associate Editor of Old Testament Articles , Samuel Terrien, Associate Editor of Old Testament Articles, and Emory Stevens Bucke, Editor, Abingdon Press]

Thurston, Bonnie Bowman. *The Widows: A Women's Ministry in the Early Church.* Minneapolis: Fortress Press, 1989.

Trigilio Jr., PhD, ThD, John, and Kenneth Brighenti, PhD. *Women in the Bible for Dummies*. Hoboken, NJ: Wiley Publishing, Inc., 2005.

Wahlberg, Rachel Conrad. *Jesus According to a Woman*. New York: Paulist Press, 1975.

Whyte, Alexander. *Bible Characters*. Grand Rapids: Zondervan Publishing House, 1967.

Wright, G. Ernest. *Great People of the Bible and How They Lived*. 1974. Reprint, Pleasantville, NY: Reader's Digest Association, 1979.